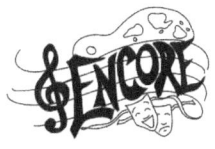

The Blue Devils Coloring Book

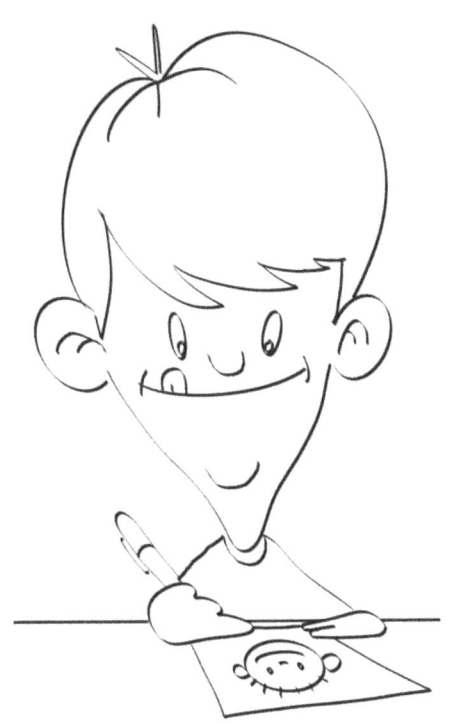

Reading, Ohio

About Encore and This Book

Encore is a group of community members from Reading, Ohio that supports artistic events and activities in the area. The Blue Devils Coloring Book brings together students, teachers, parents, and local artists in the collection of illustrations for you to color. 100% of the profits from the sale of this book go toward furthering artistic development in Reading in the form of performances, clubs, supplies, and events for kids and adults. For more information, visit us on Twitter and Instagram @ReadingEncore, or email us at EncoreReading@gmail.com

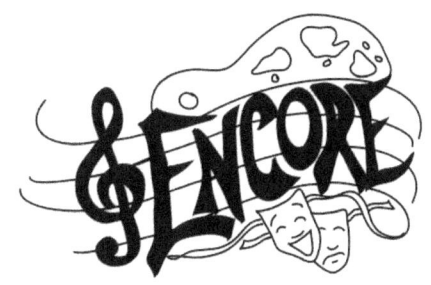

Encore: Supporting the Arts in Reading

Puppy's Dream

Kyleigh Roberts and
Misty Fischer
4th grade and Parent

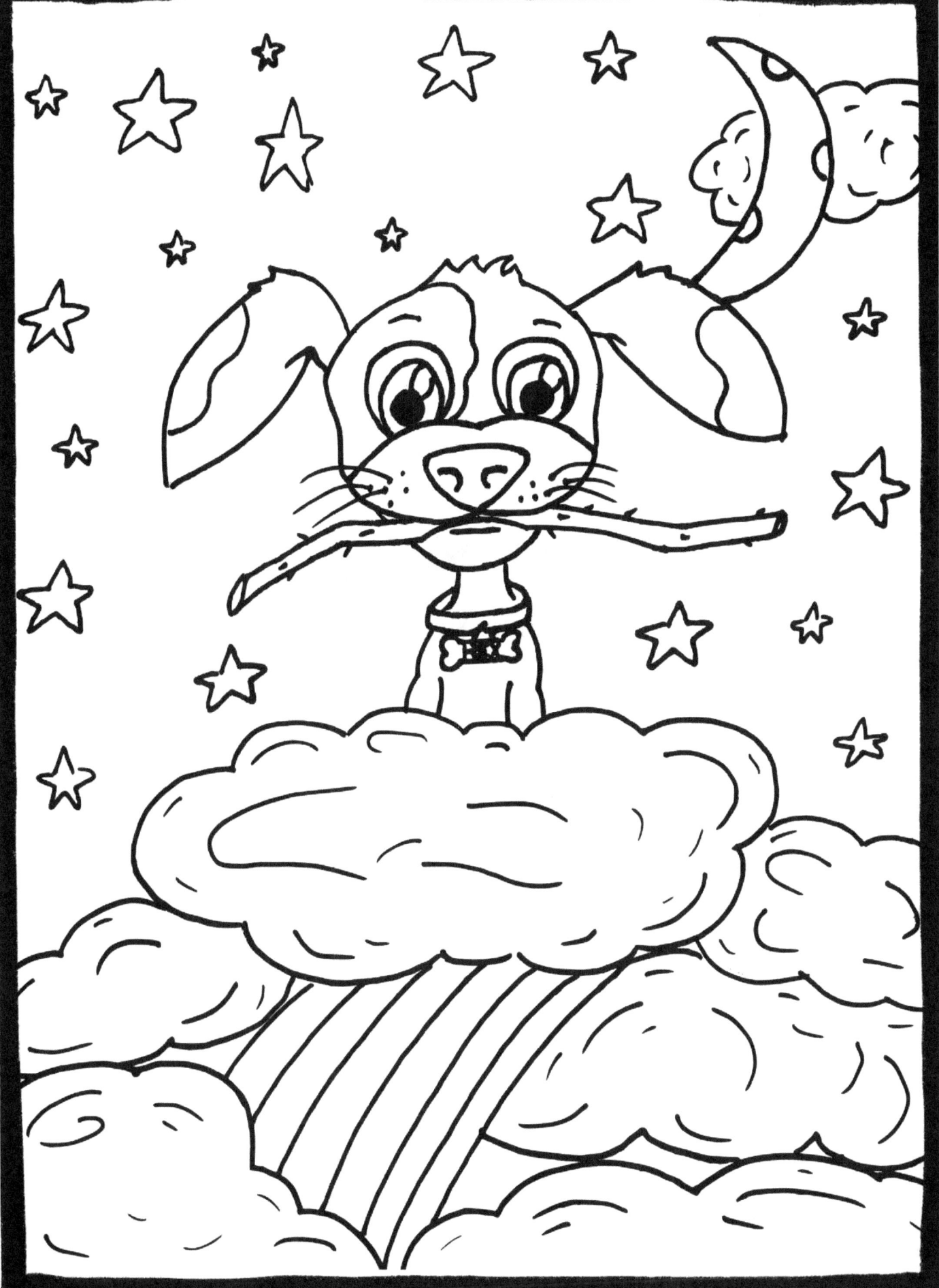

City Song
Katie Altman
8th grade

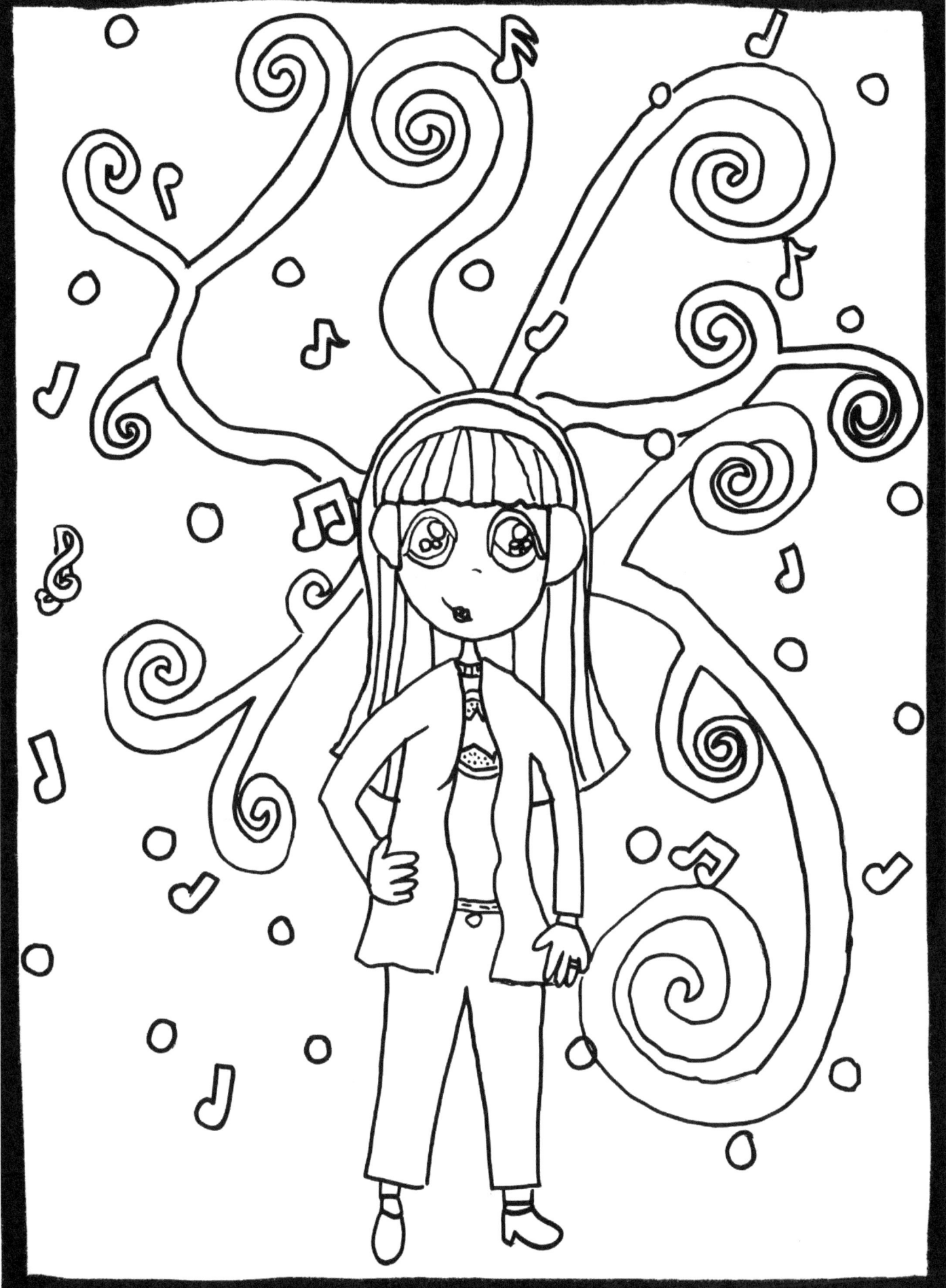

Roses and Stuff
Katelynn Mrusek
11th grade

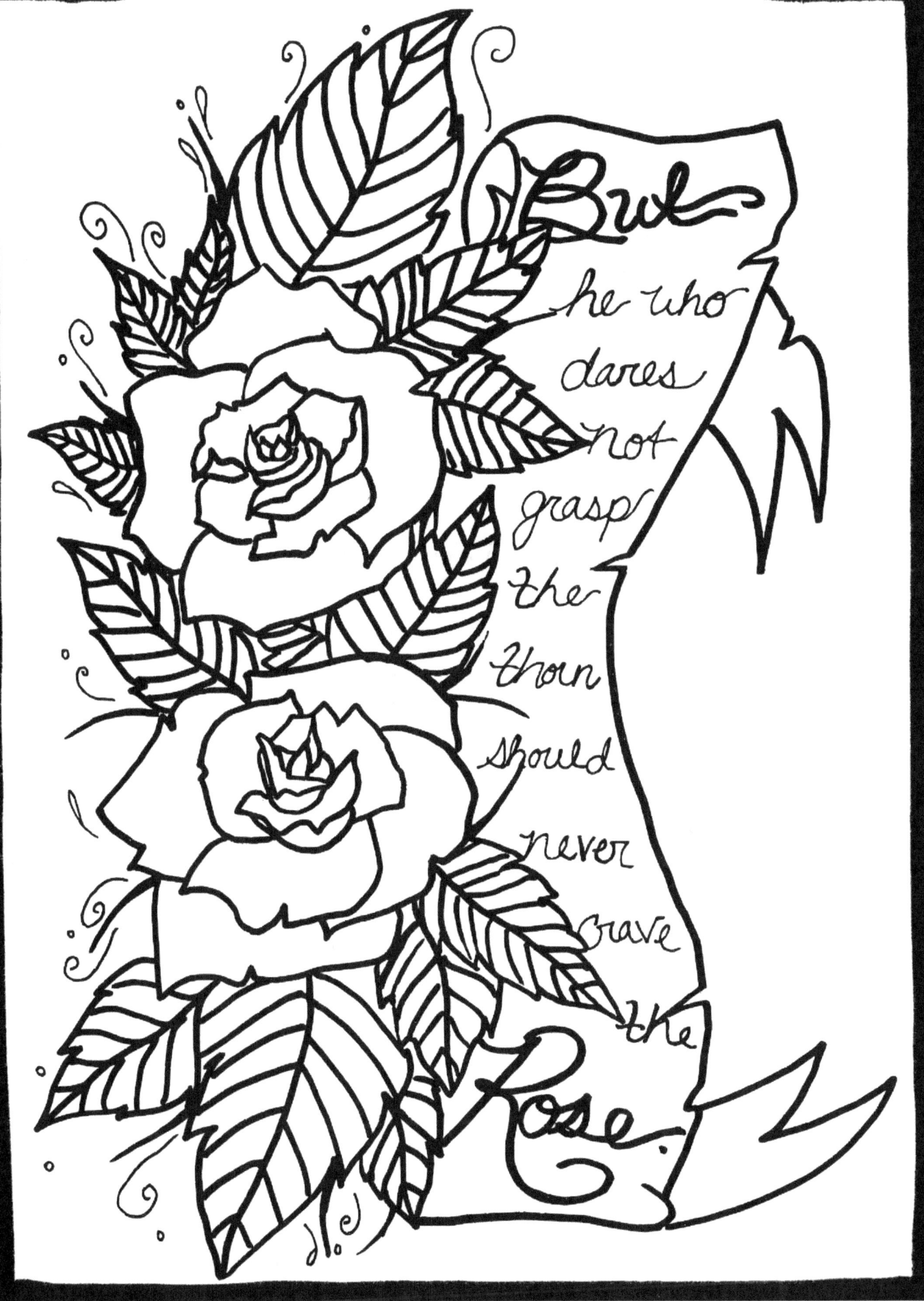

Cutie Life
Avery Bose
2nd grade

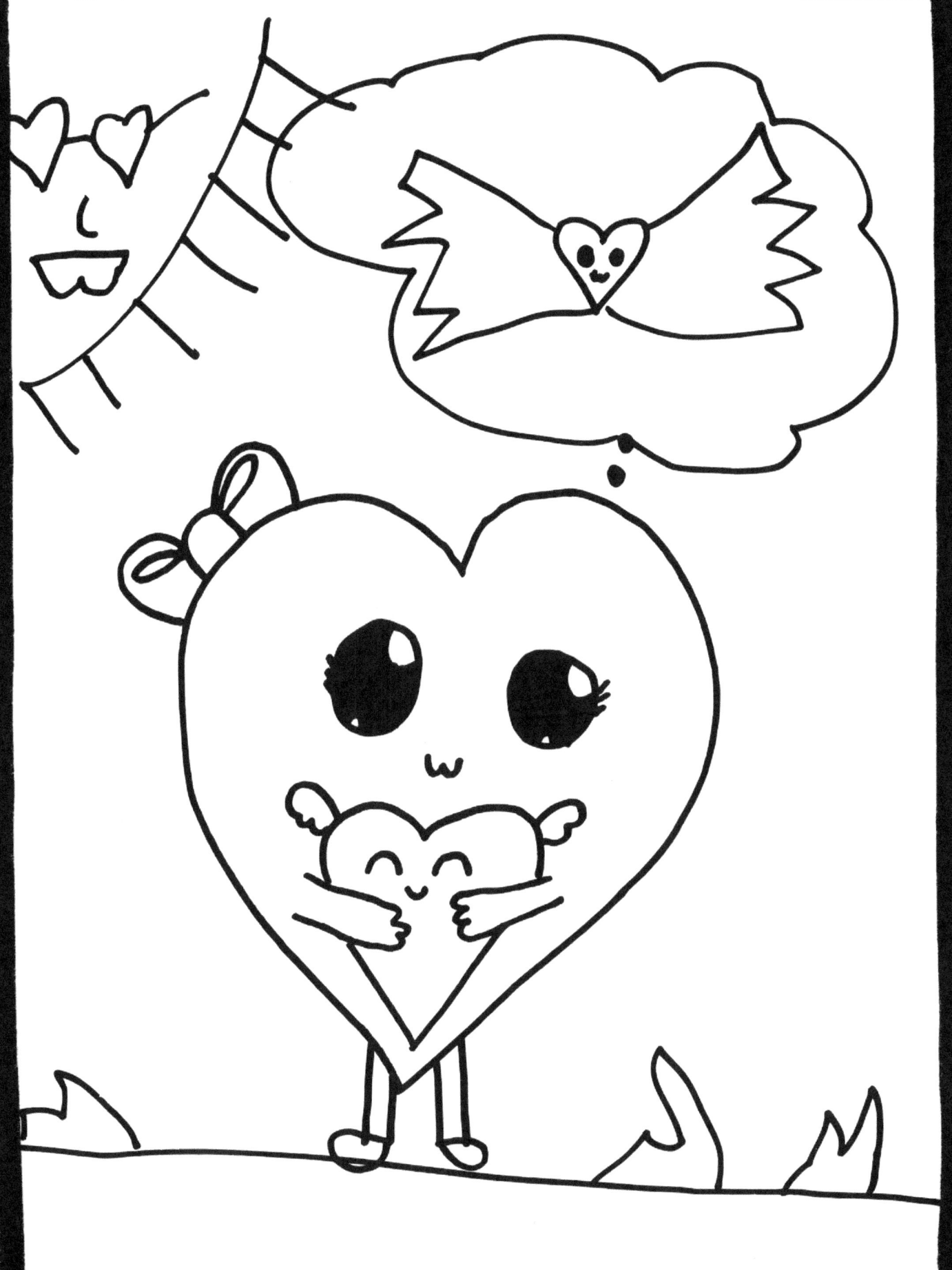

Ella the Donut

Annalise Street
4th grade

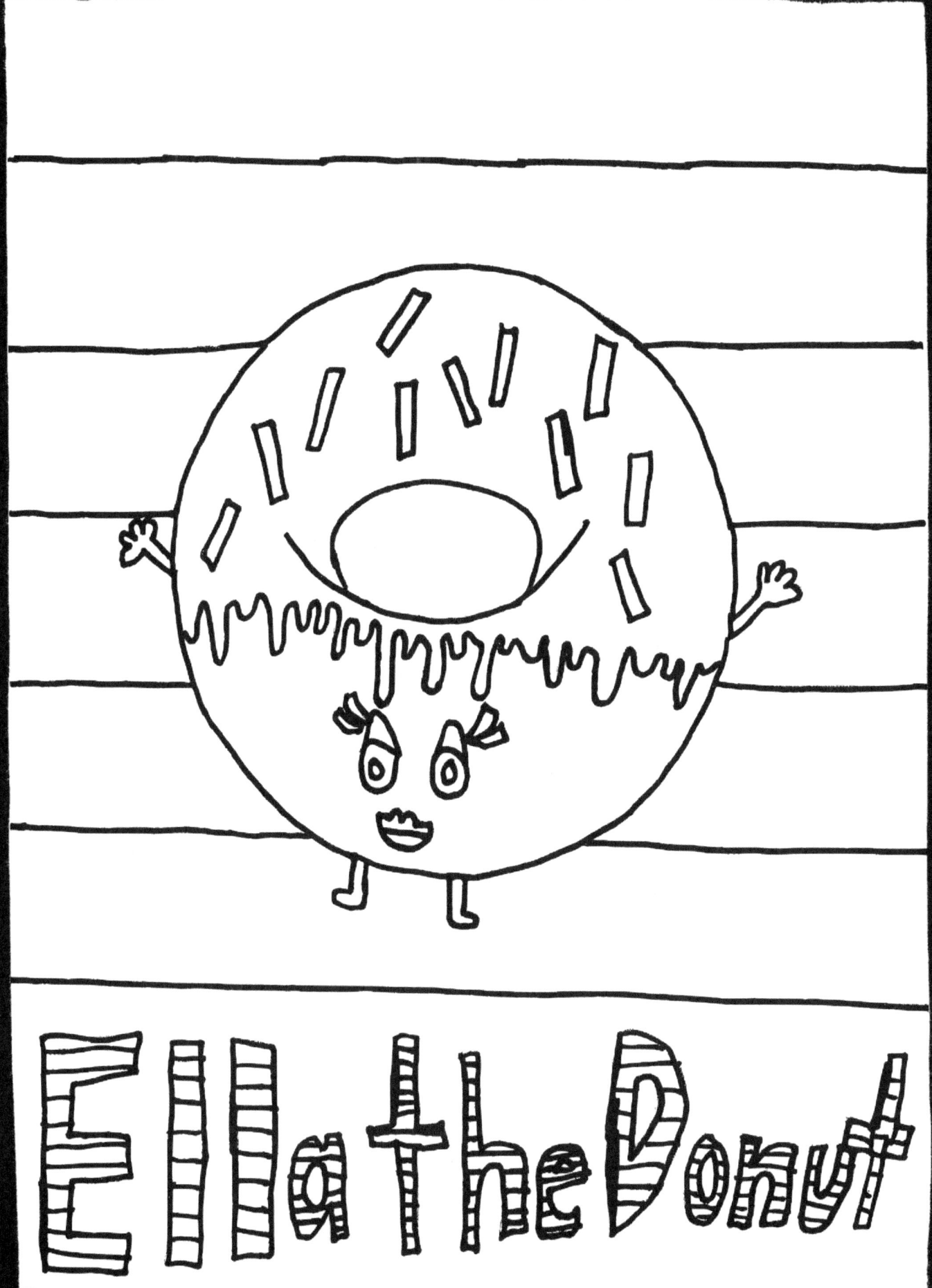

Ted the Conehead

Benny Hess
7th grade

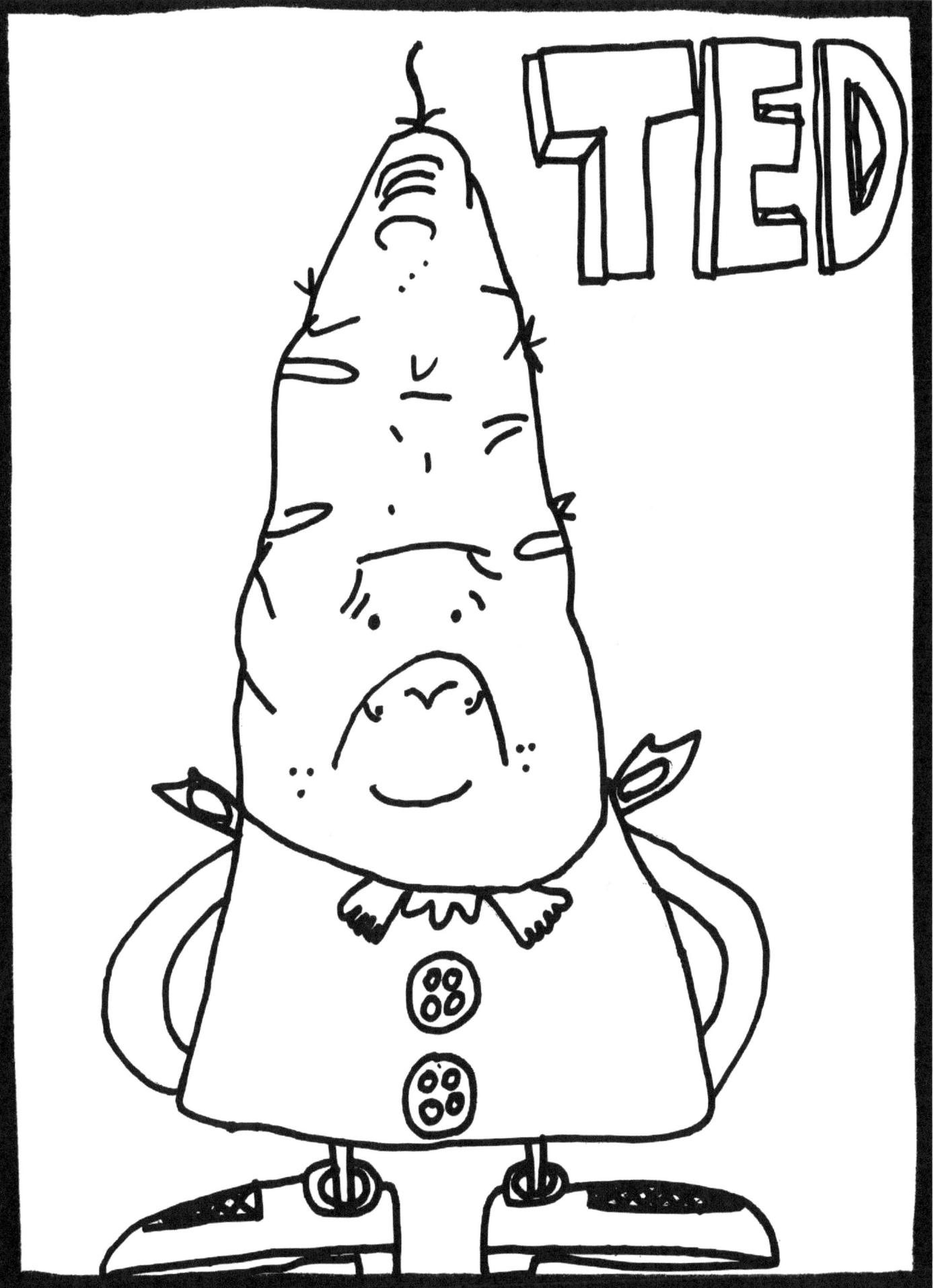

Owl's Idea

Heather Pare
5th grade

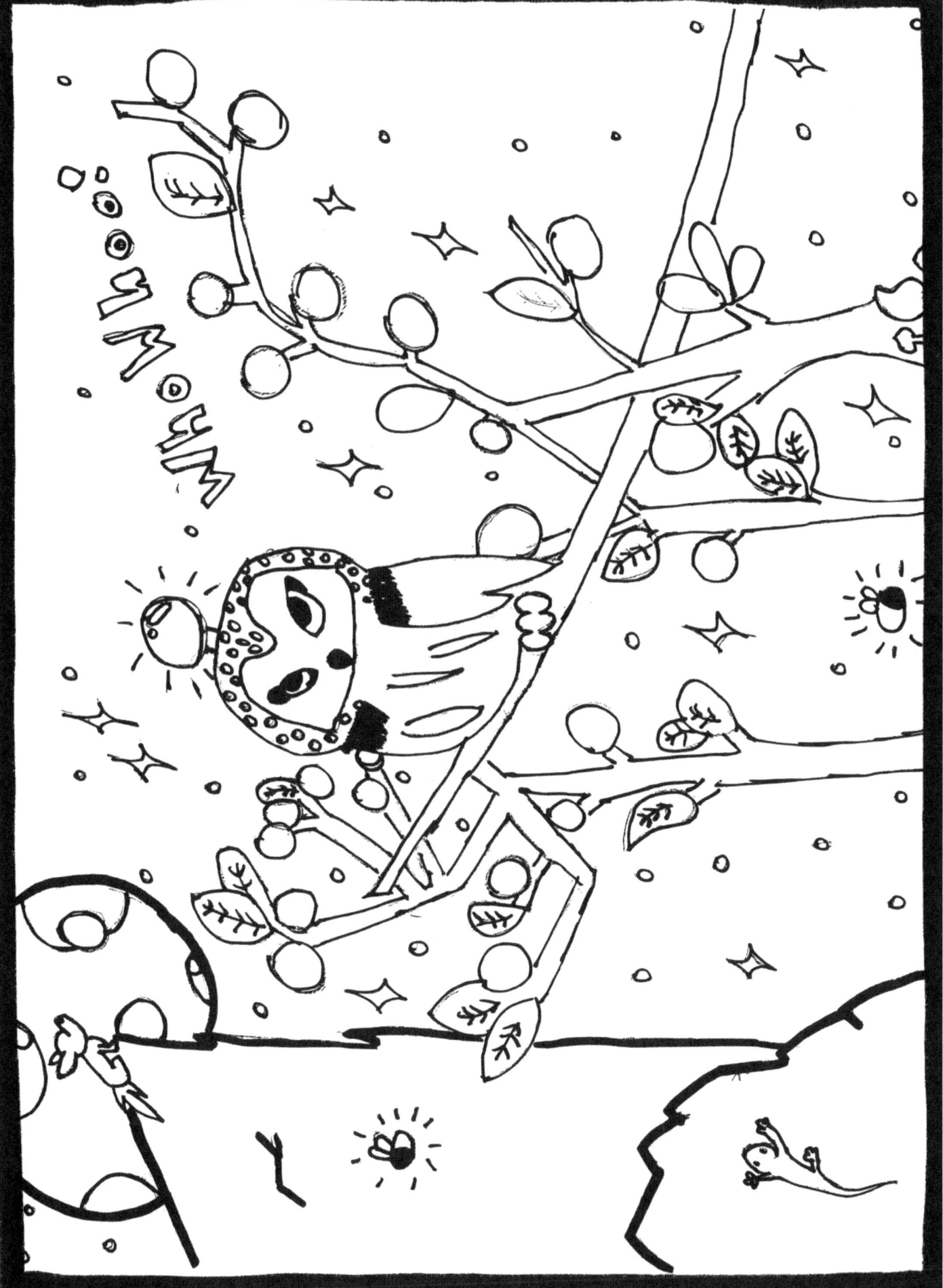

Teach Monster
Mrs. Willman
Elementary Tech Tools

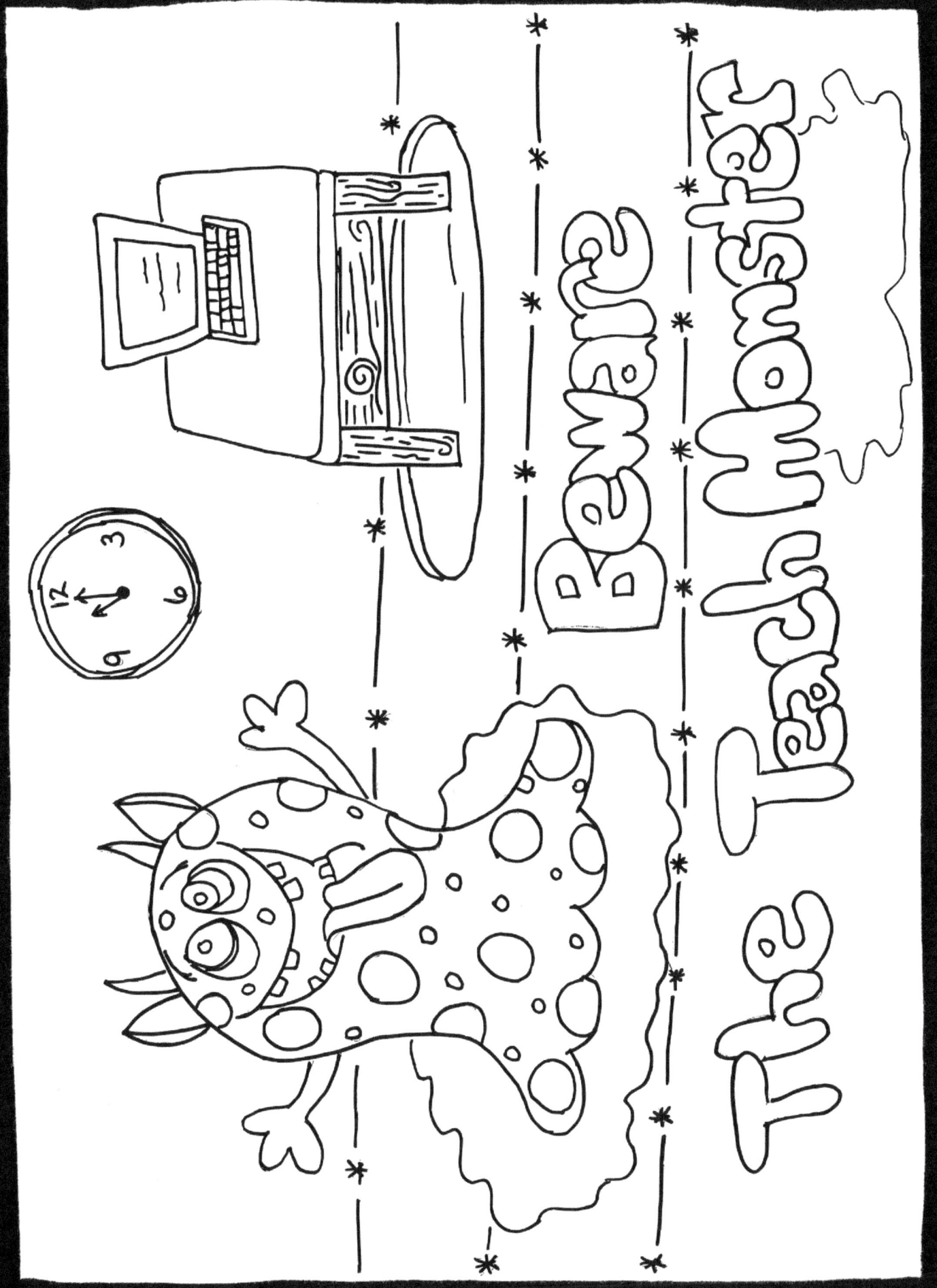

An Angel Cat
Bree Ridner
5th grade

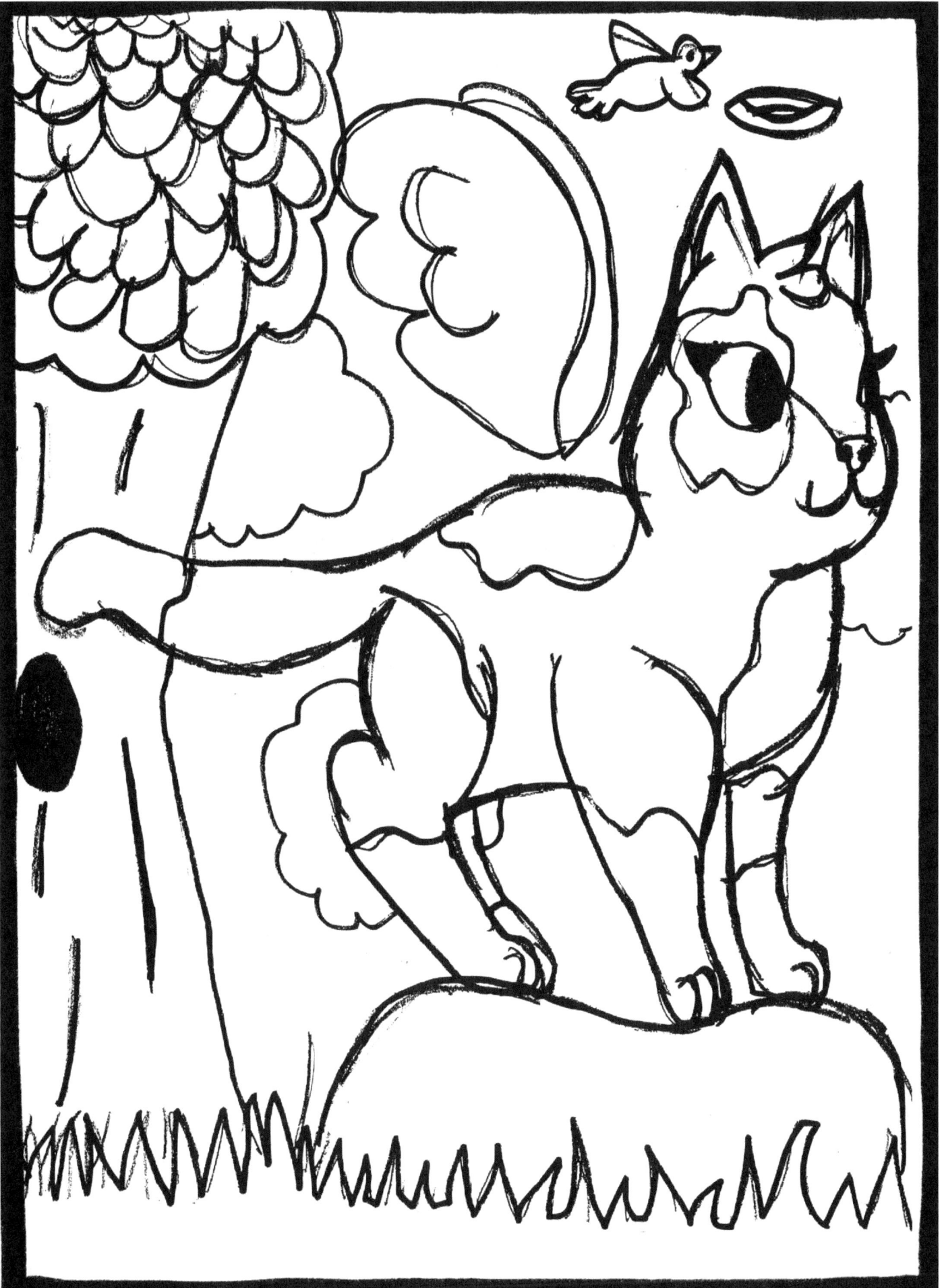

Hole in the Wall

Skylynn Recker
7th grade

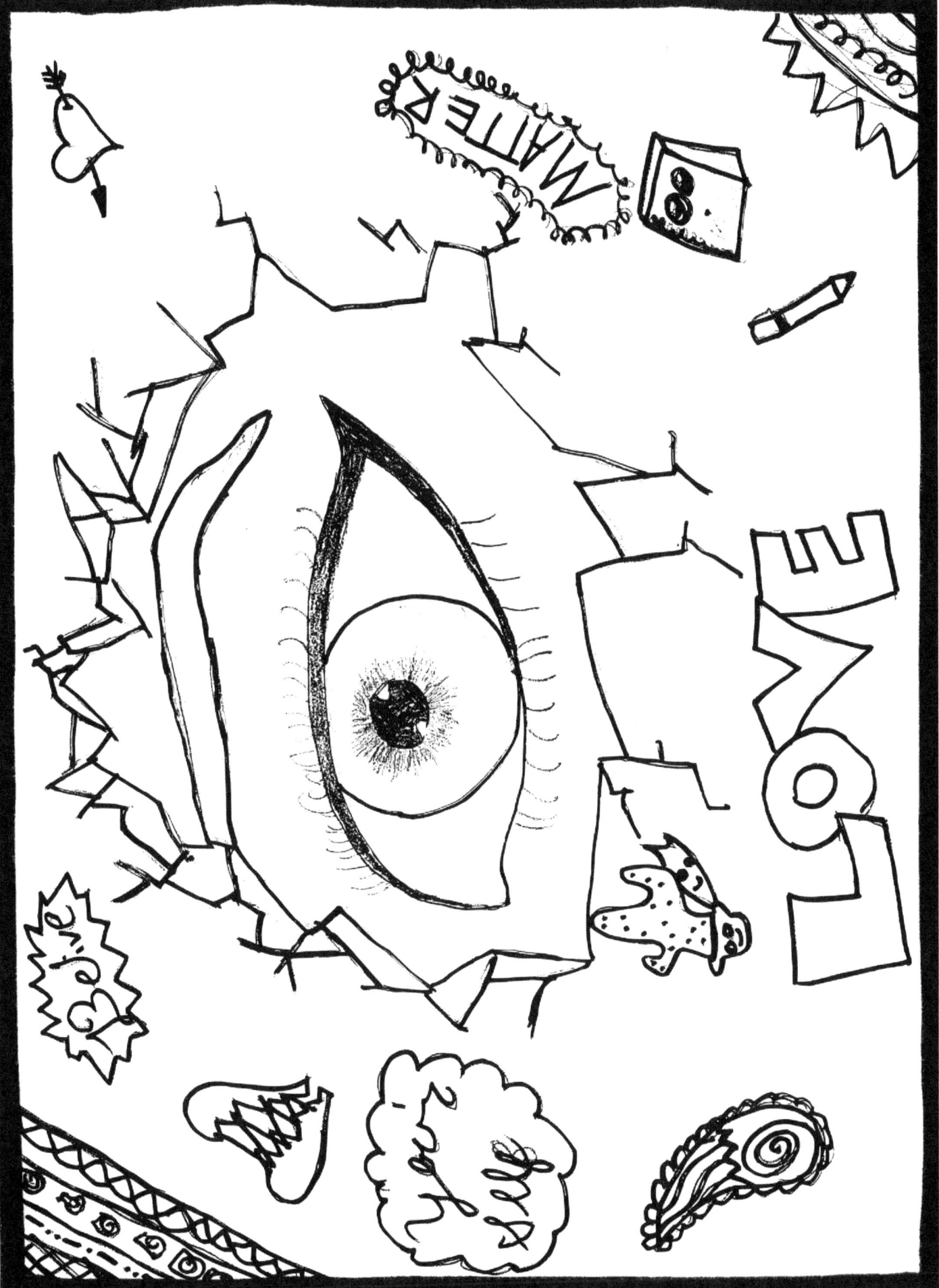

Lilly the Dog

Hannah Chandler
5th grade

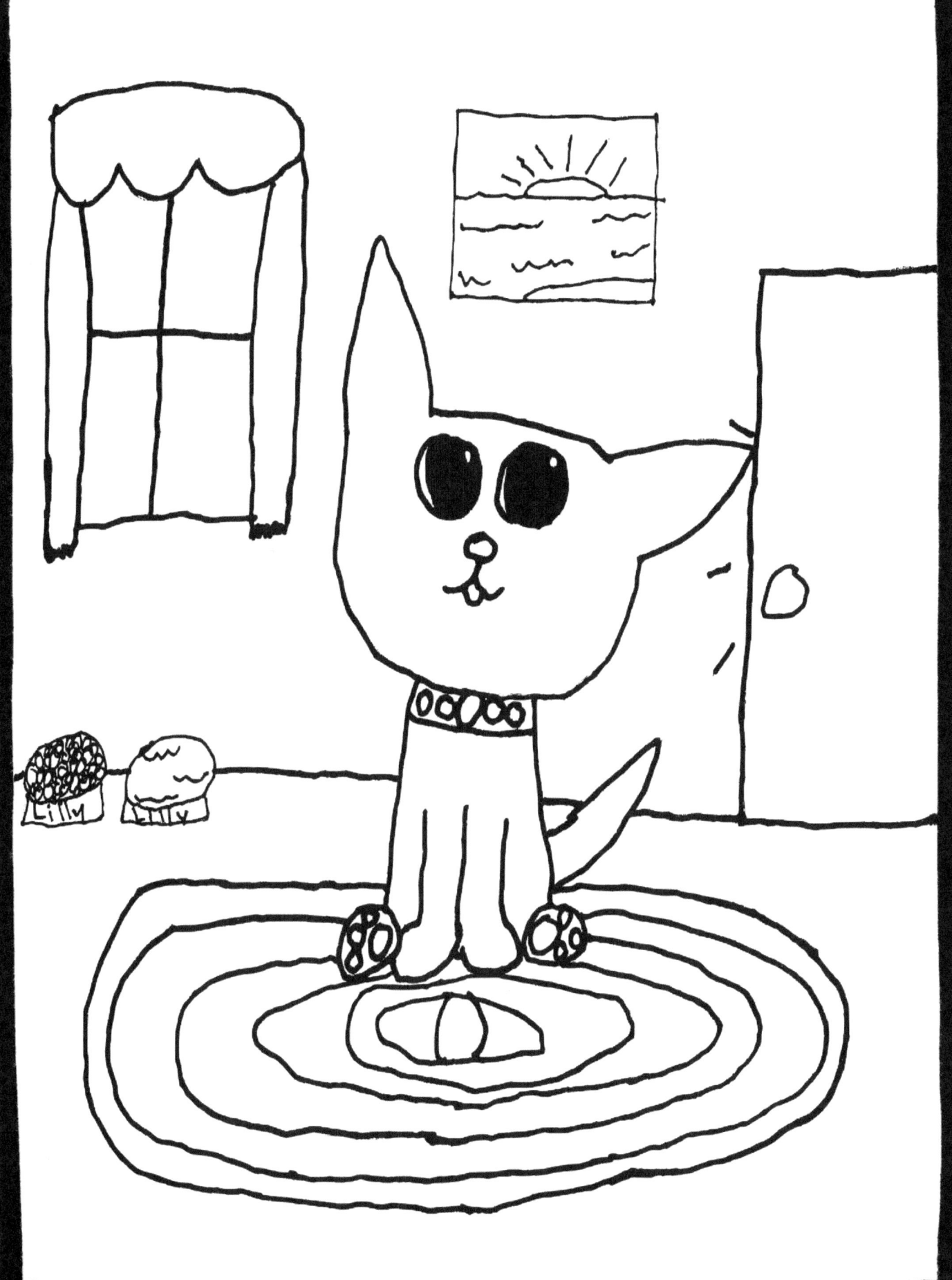

Robot
Mike Altman
Parent and Local
Artist

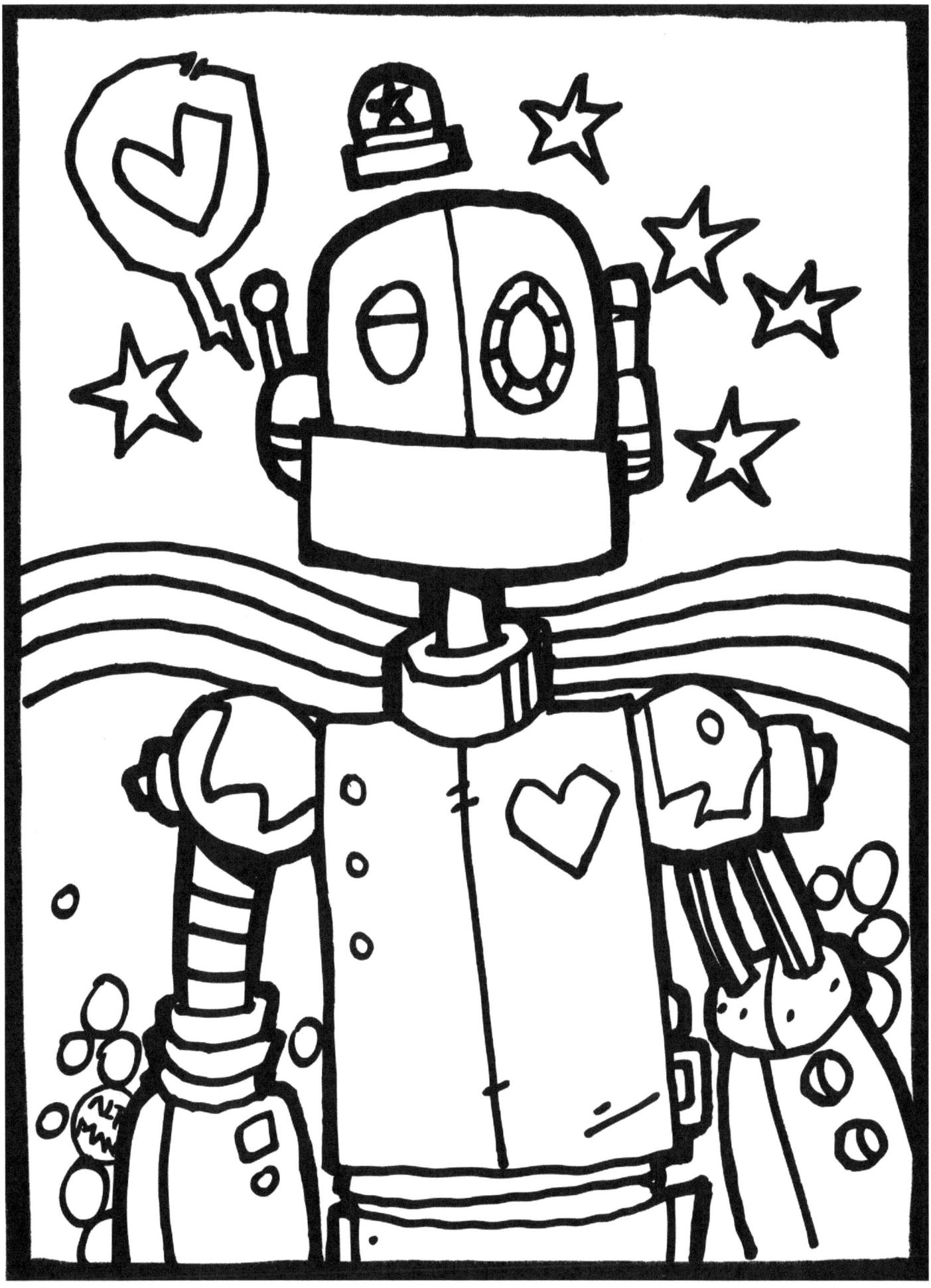

A New Encounter

Italy Downs
5th grade

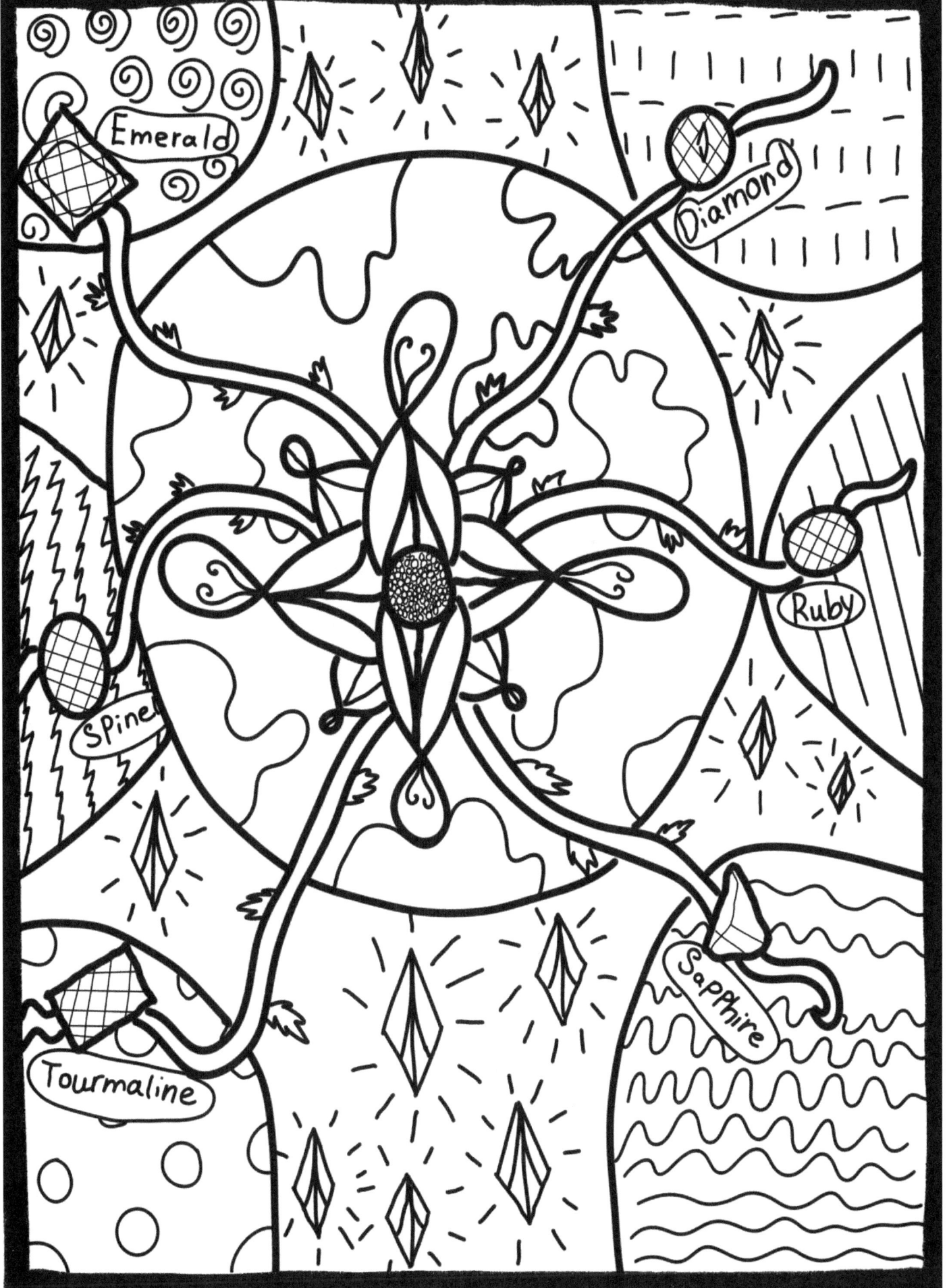

Untitled

Meadow Kerlin
10th grade

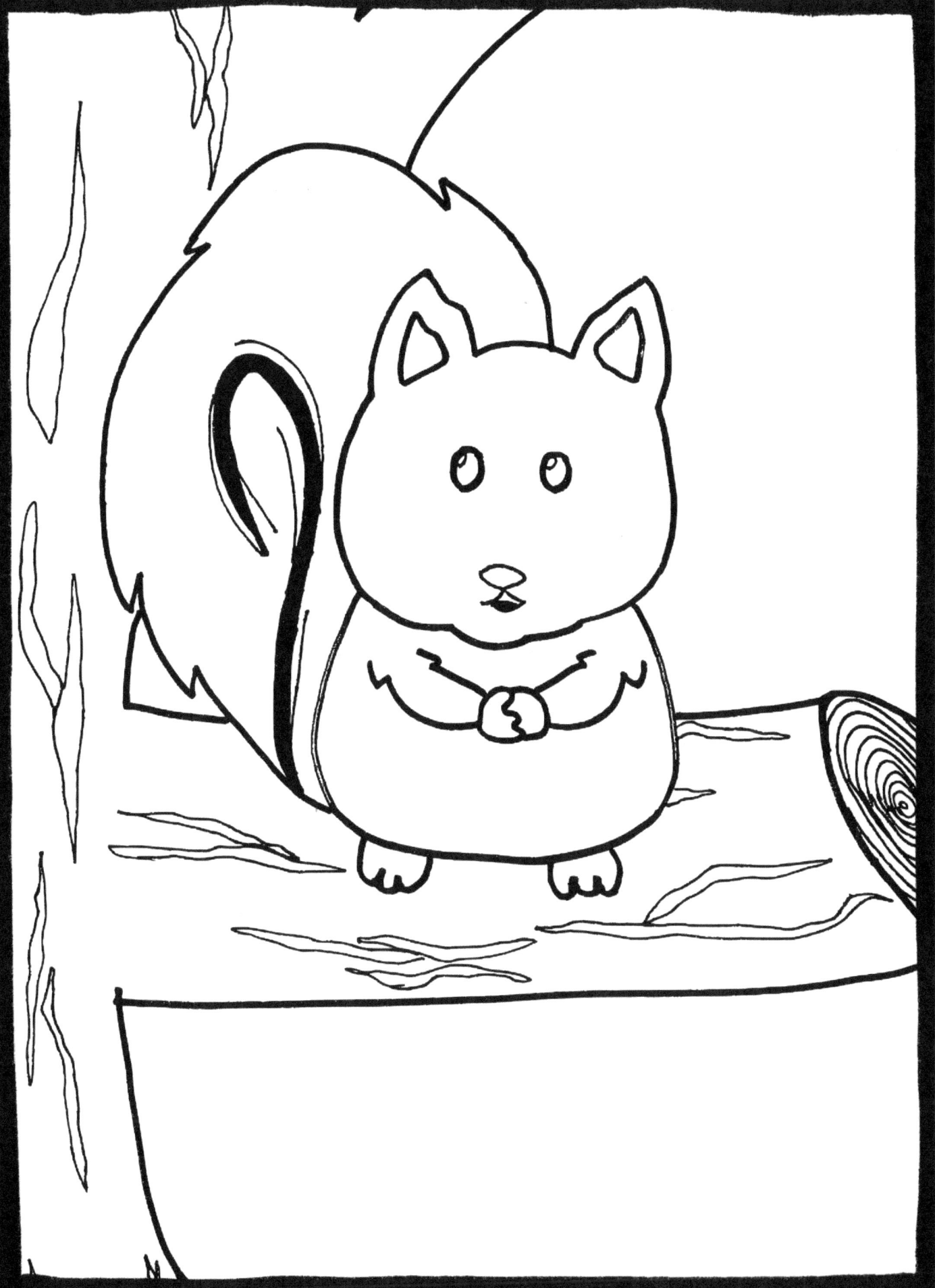

The Dots at Fenway Park

Mr. Hayes
5th grade Teacher

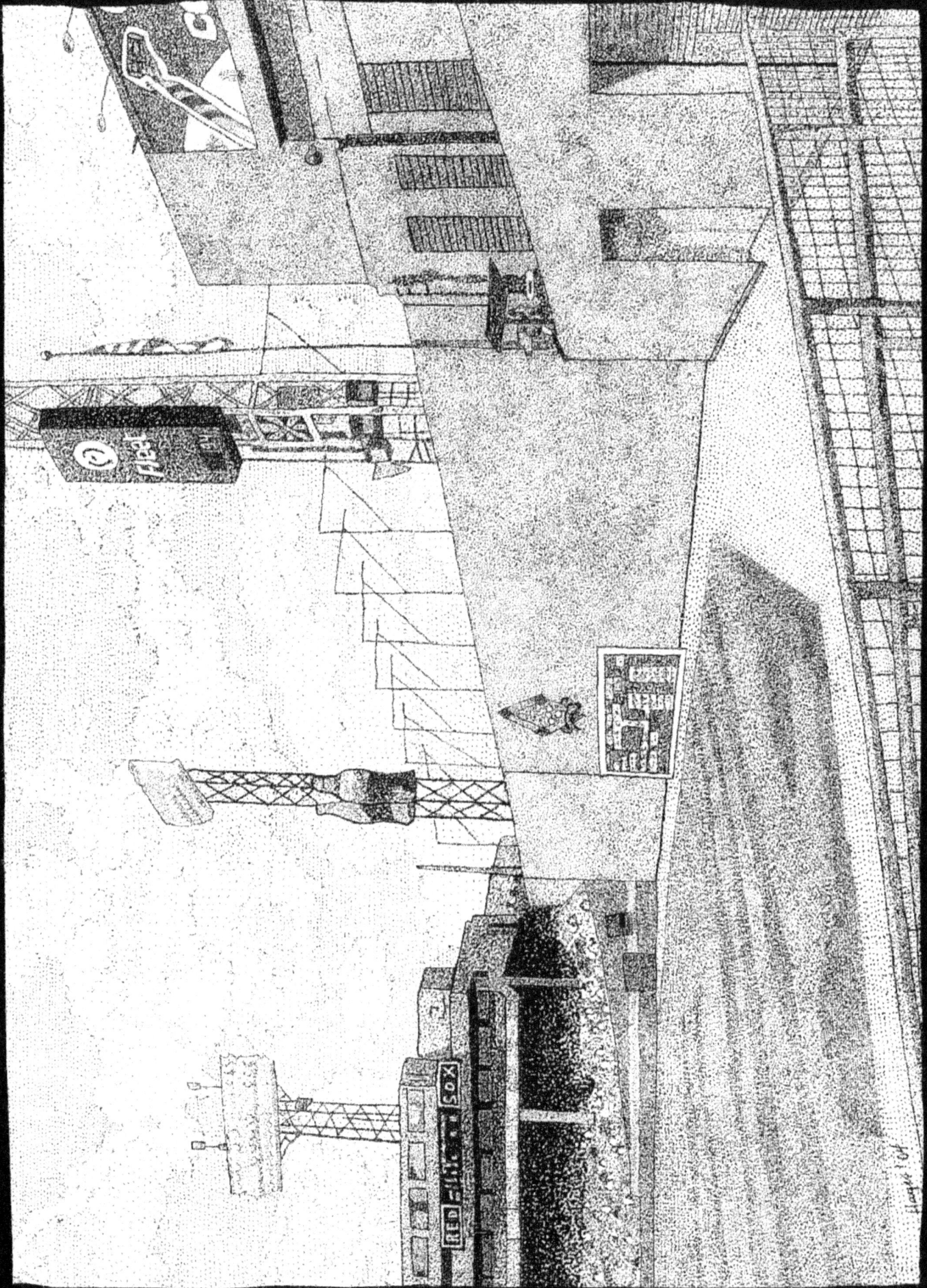

Unicorn Universe

Samantha Dyer
5th grade

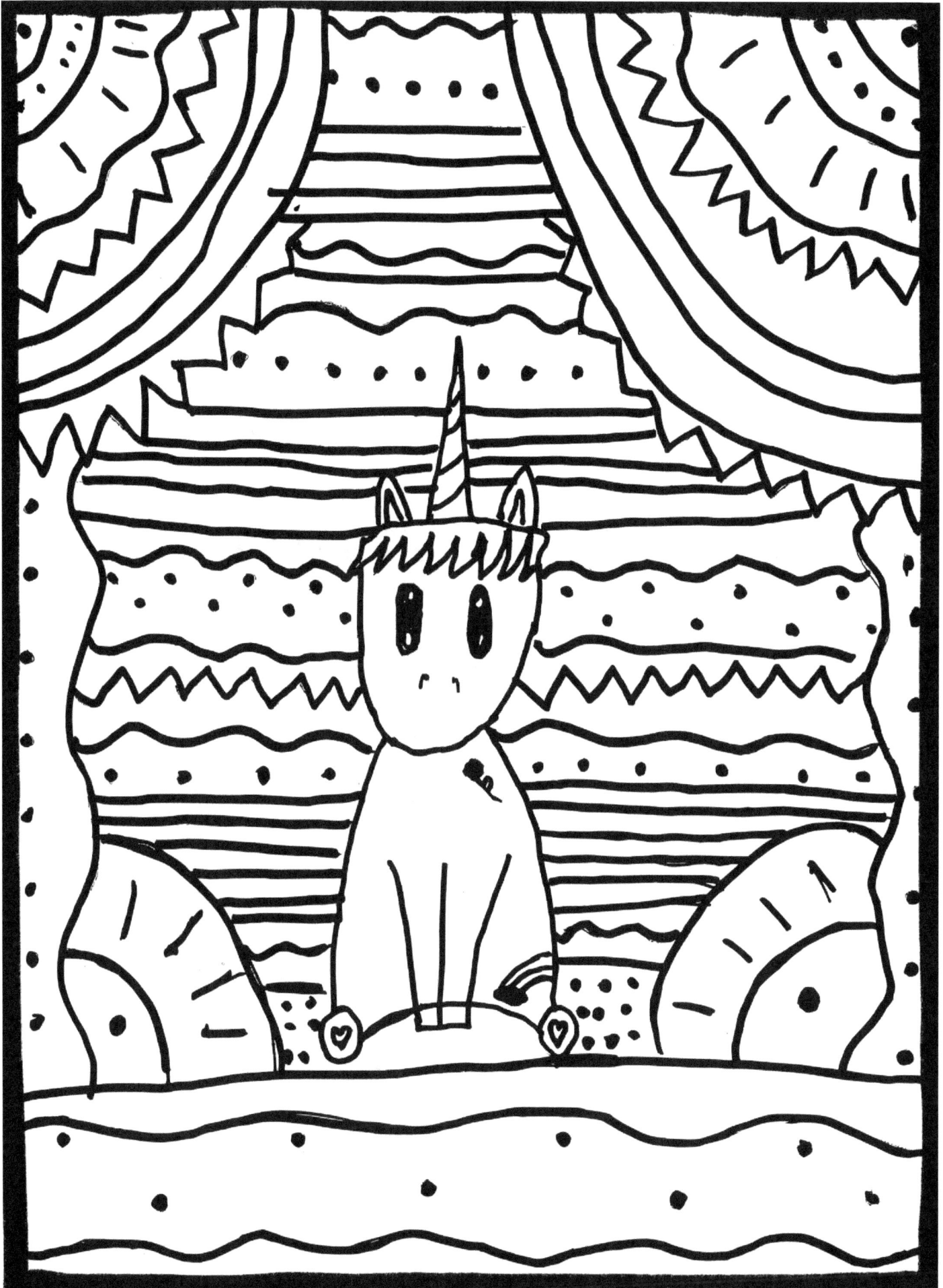

Bee Great, Pollinate

Ms. Dehner
Middle and High School Art

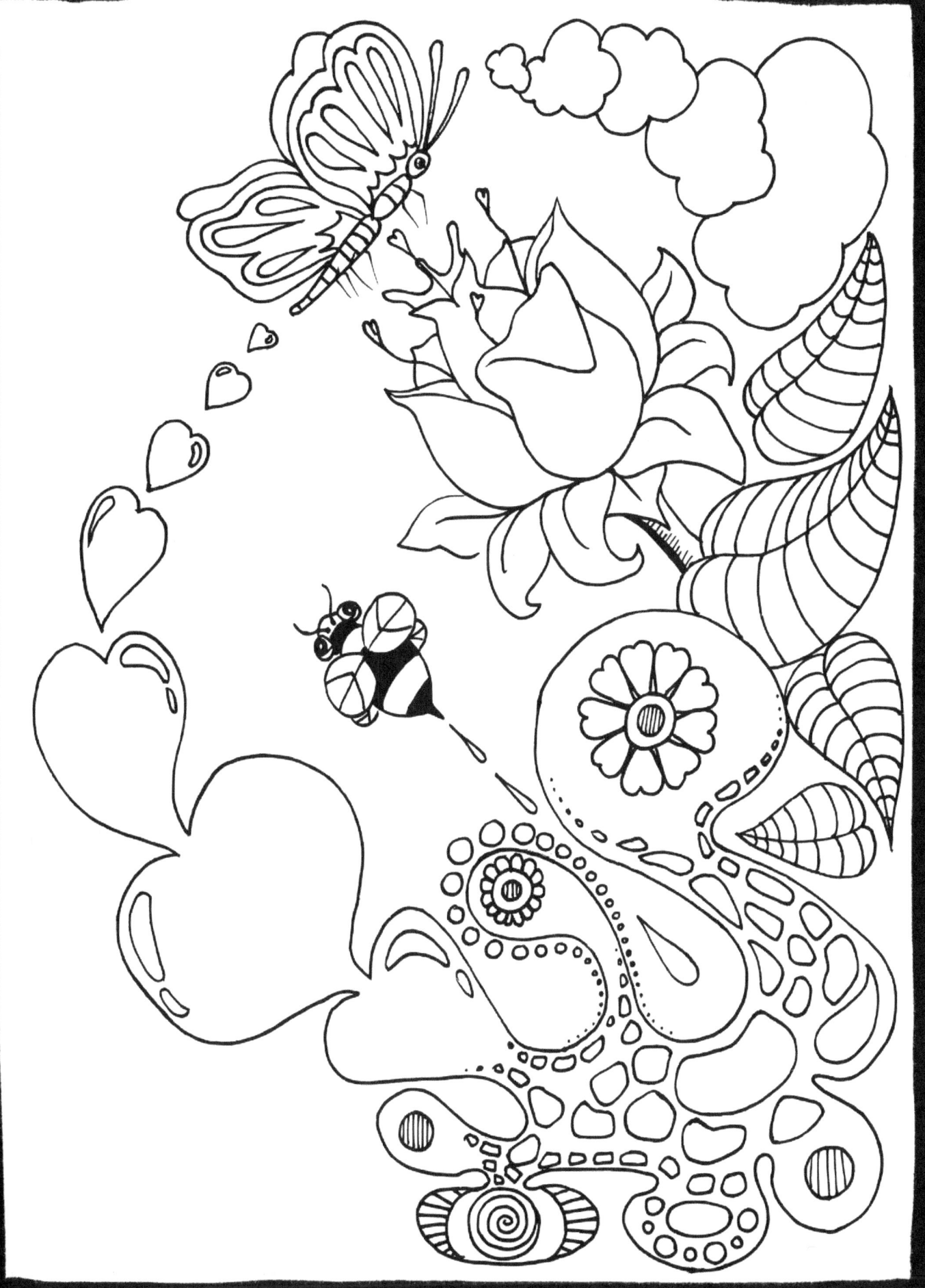

The Lollipop Army

Cailey Ridner

8th grade

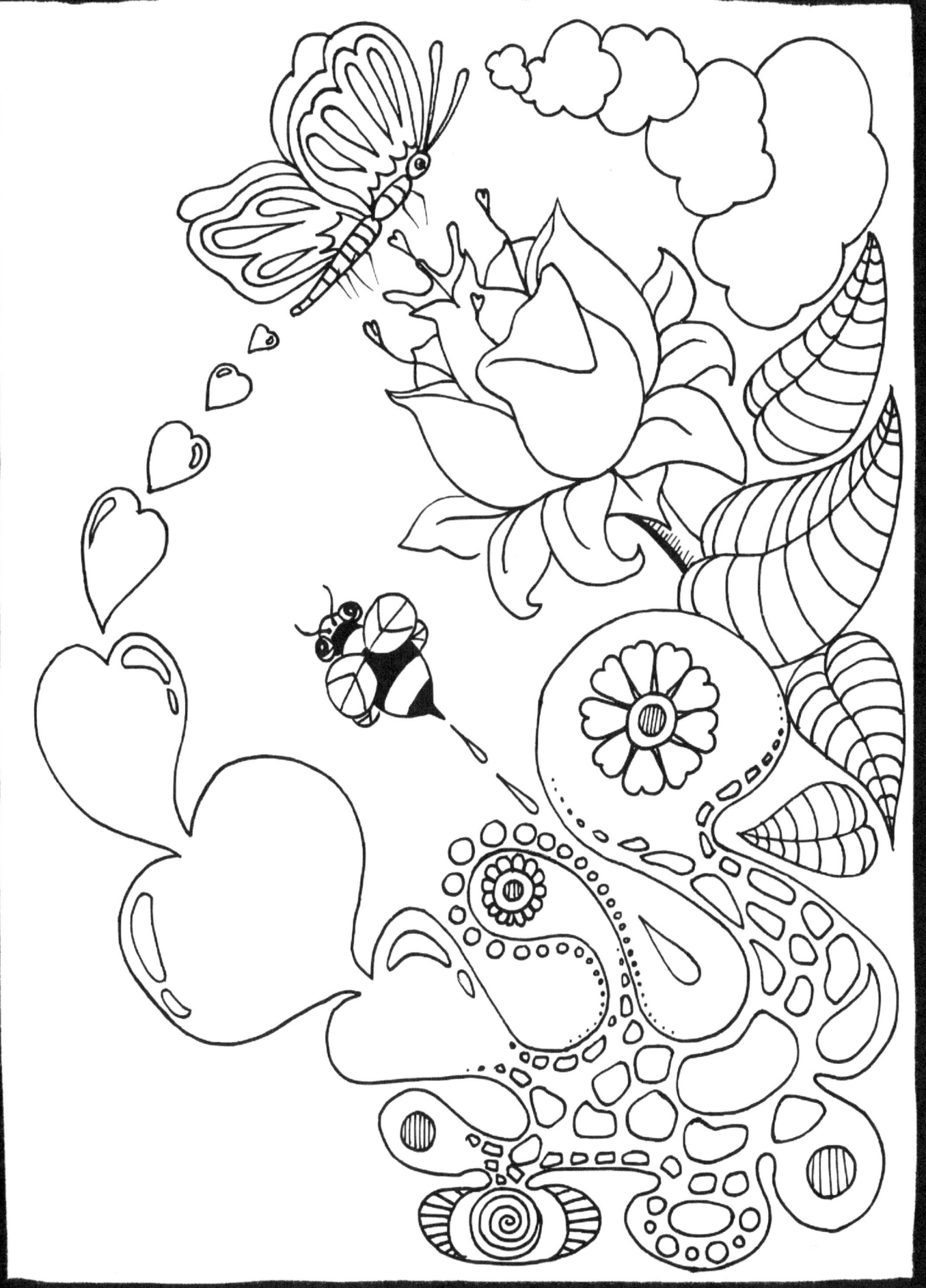

The Lollipop Army
Cailey Ridner
8th grade

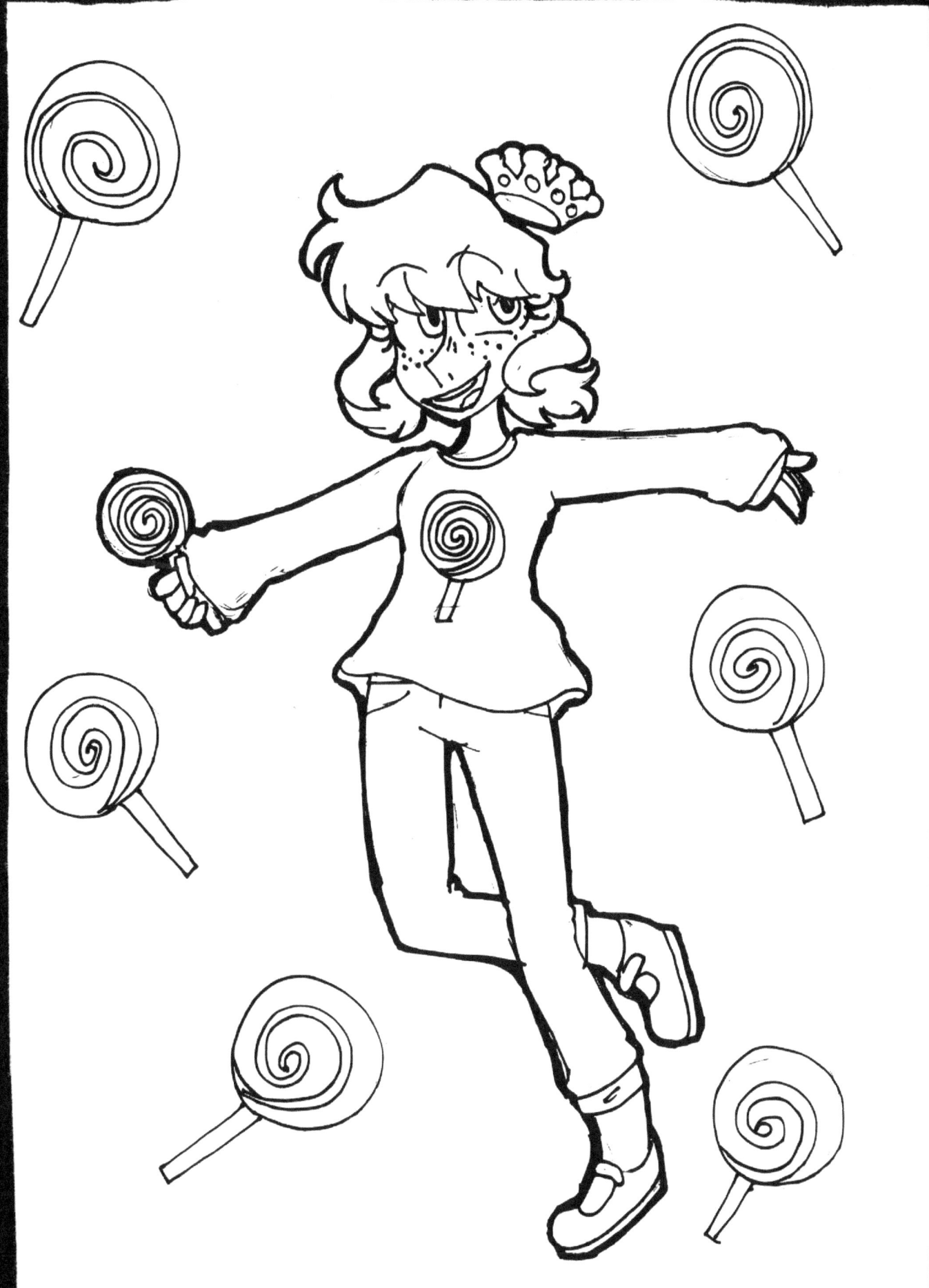

The Pride of Reading
Mr. Kamerer
Elementary PE

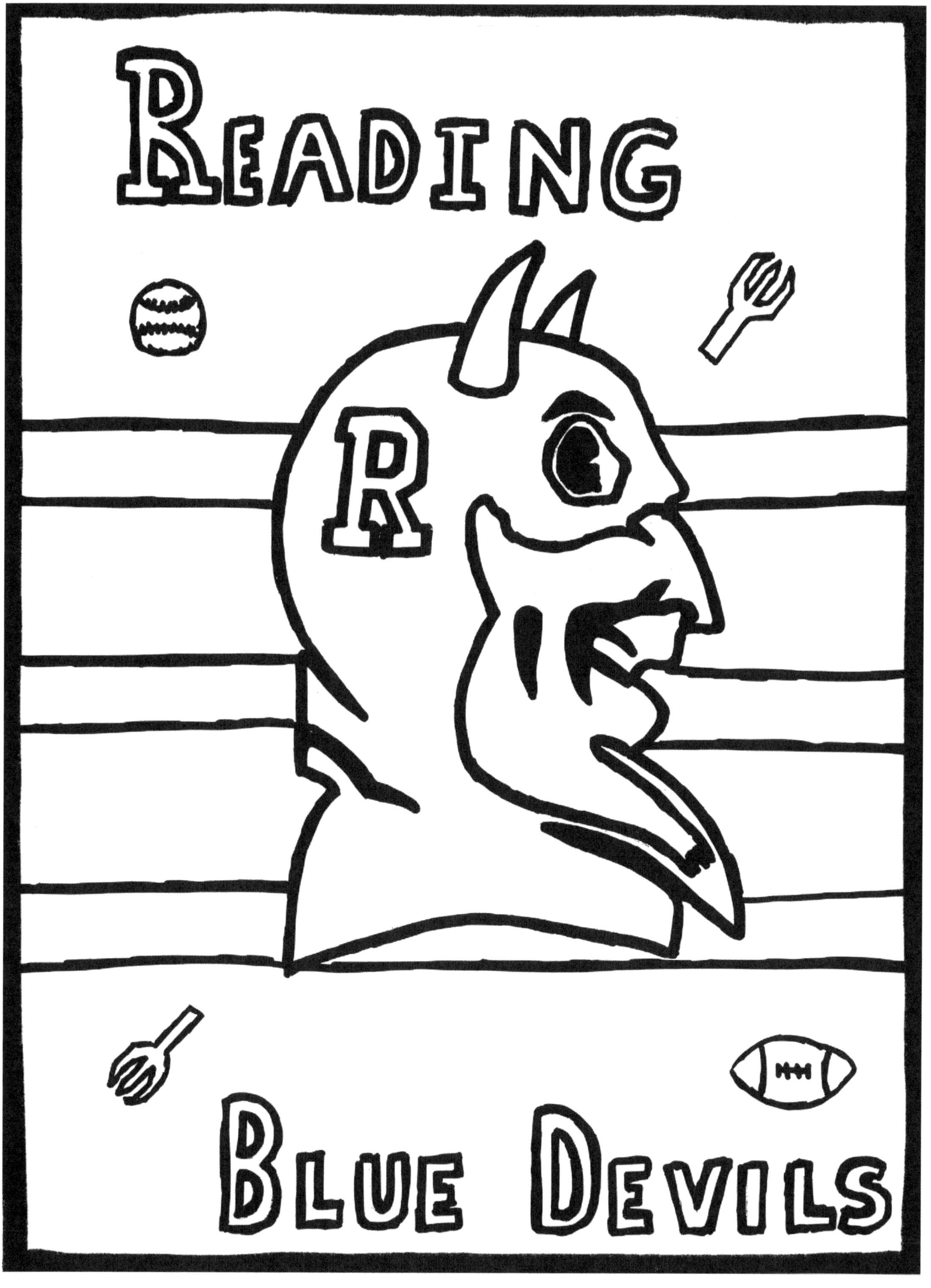

Reading
Blue Devils

Basketball

Drew Vondermeulen
7th grade

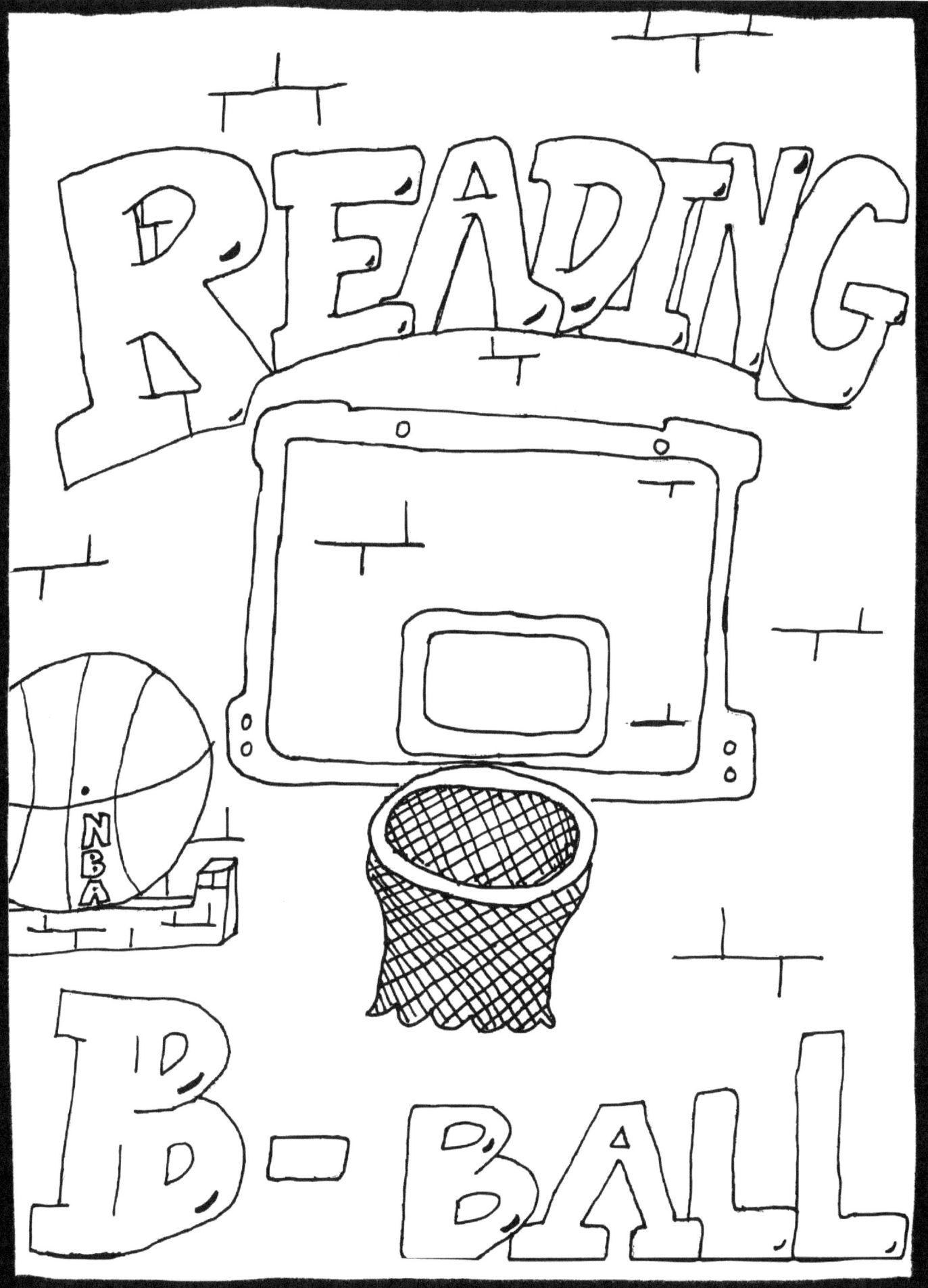

Lady Frog
Jordan Cain
2nd grade

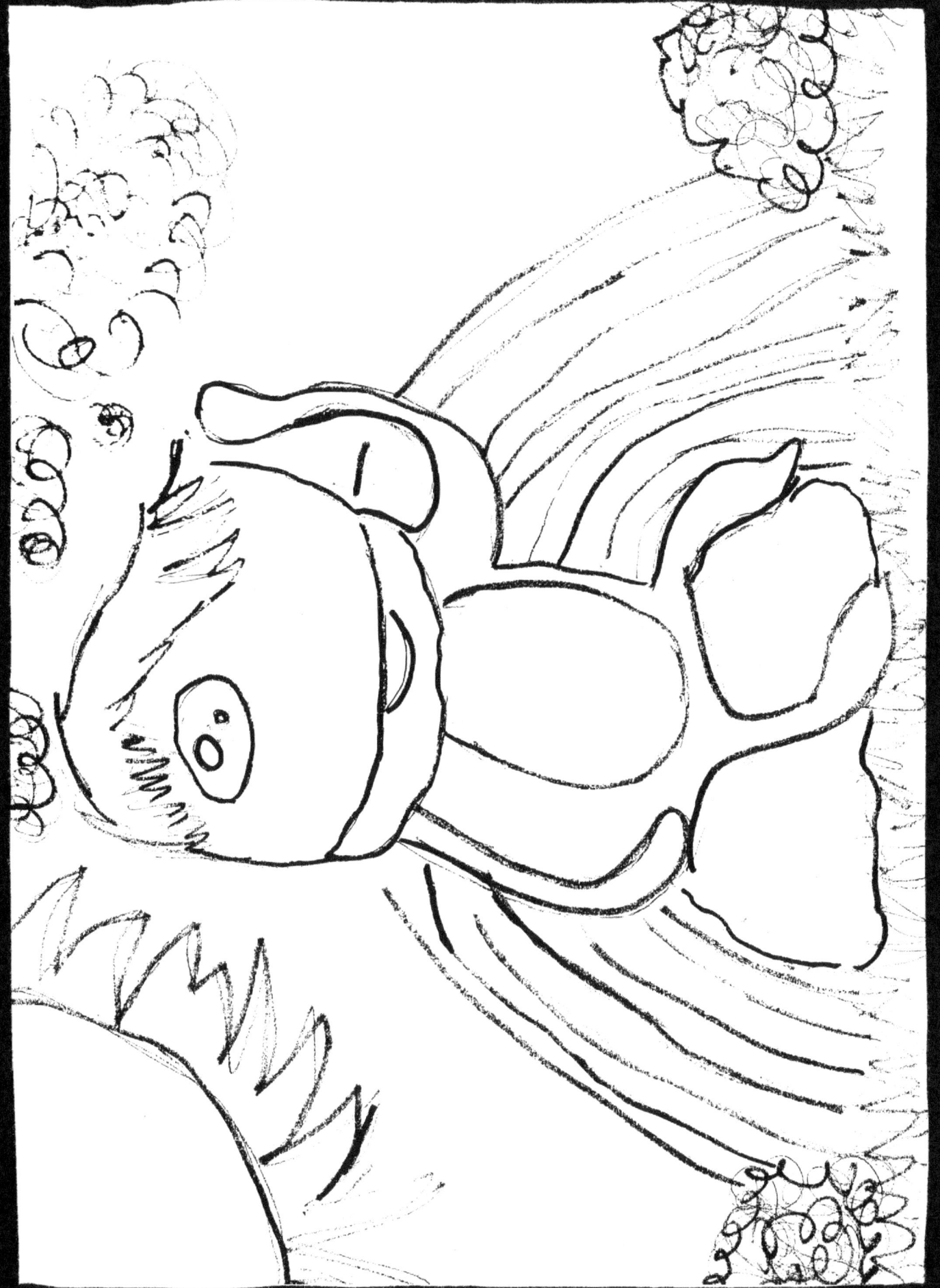

How You Doing?
Mrs. Blair
Hilltop Counselor

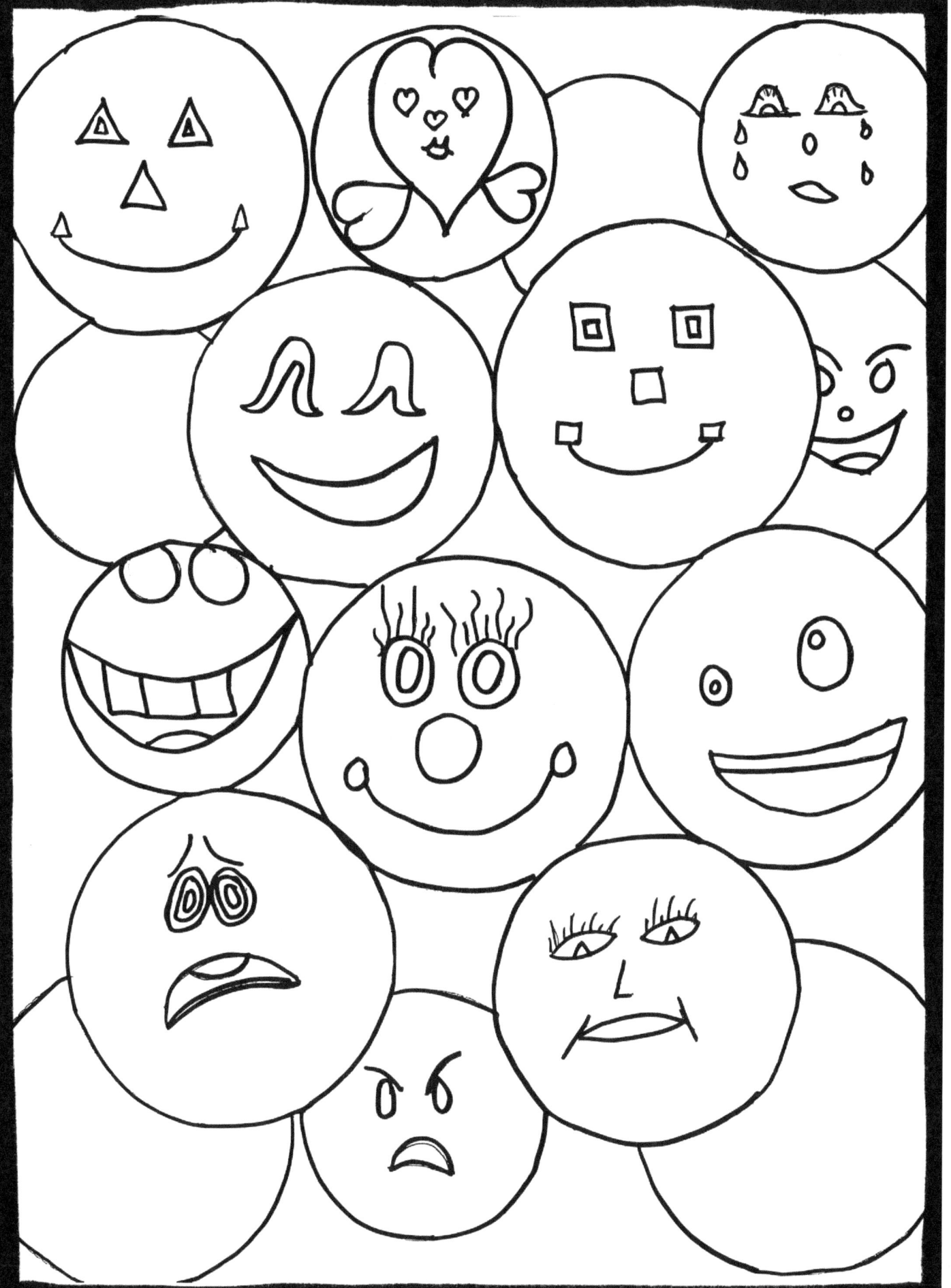

Hope
Sage Altman
6th grade

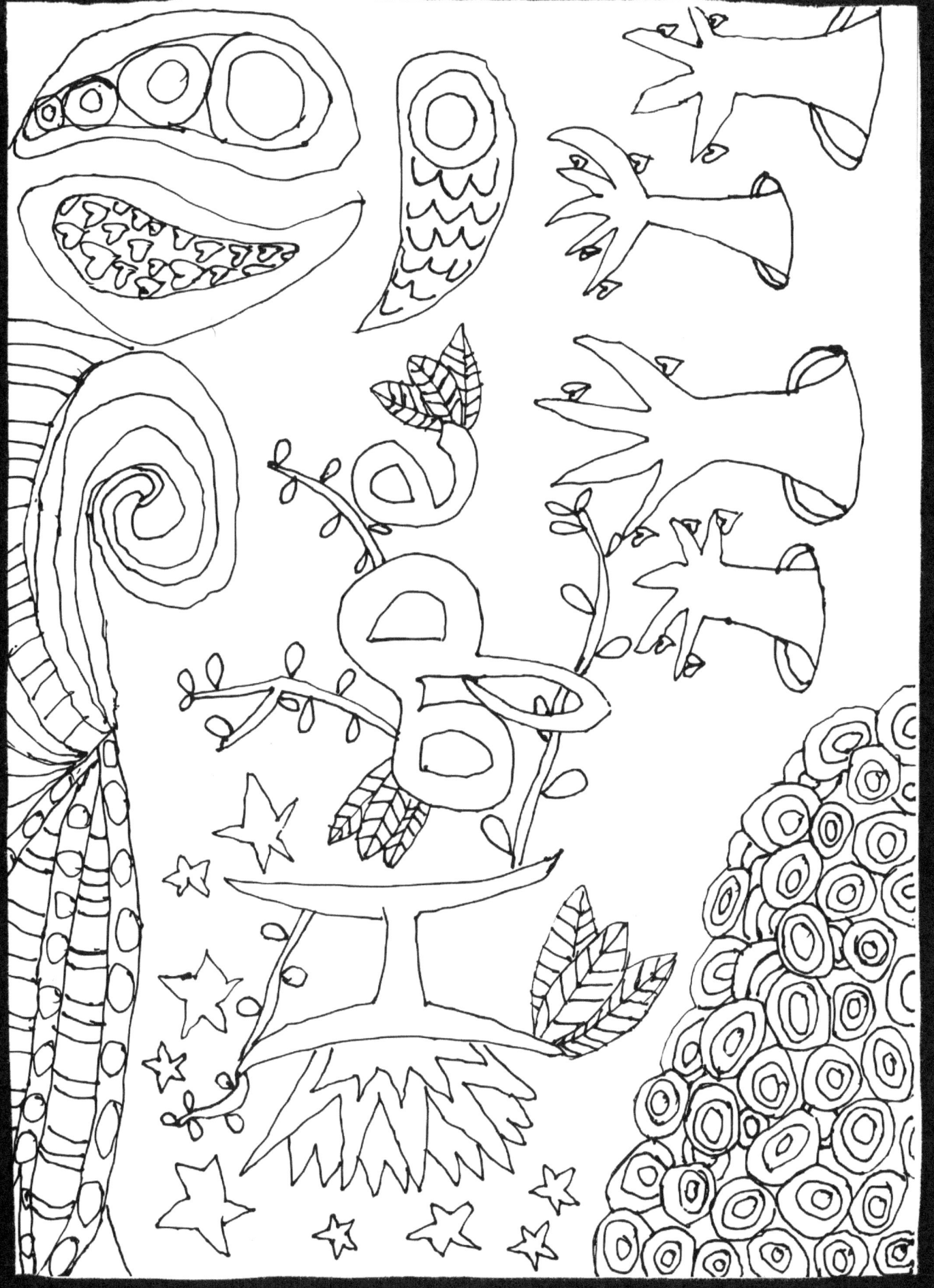

Musical Whims
Mr. Clark
Elementary Music

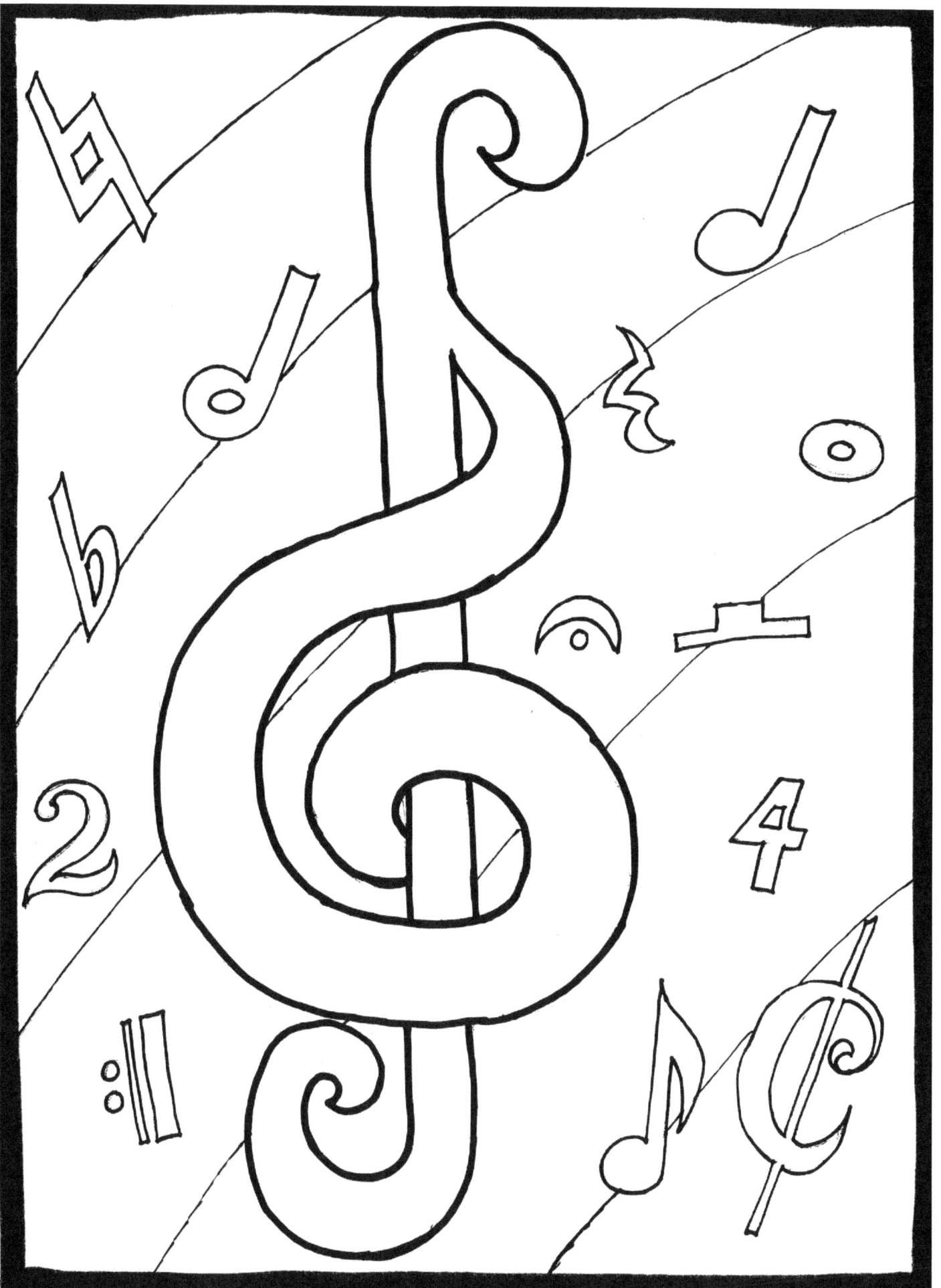

Eye Have My Eyes on You

Lorena Zander

4th grade

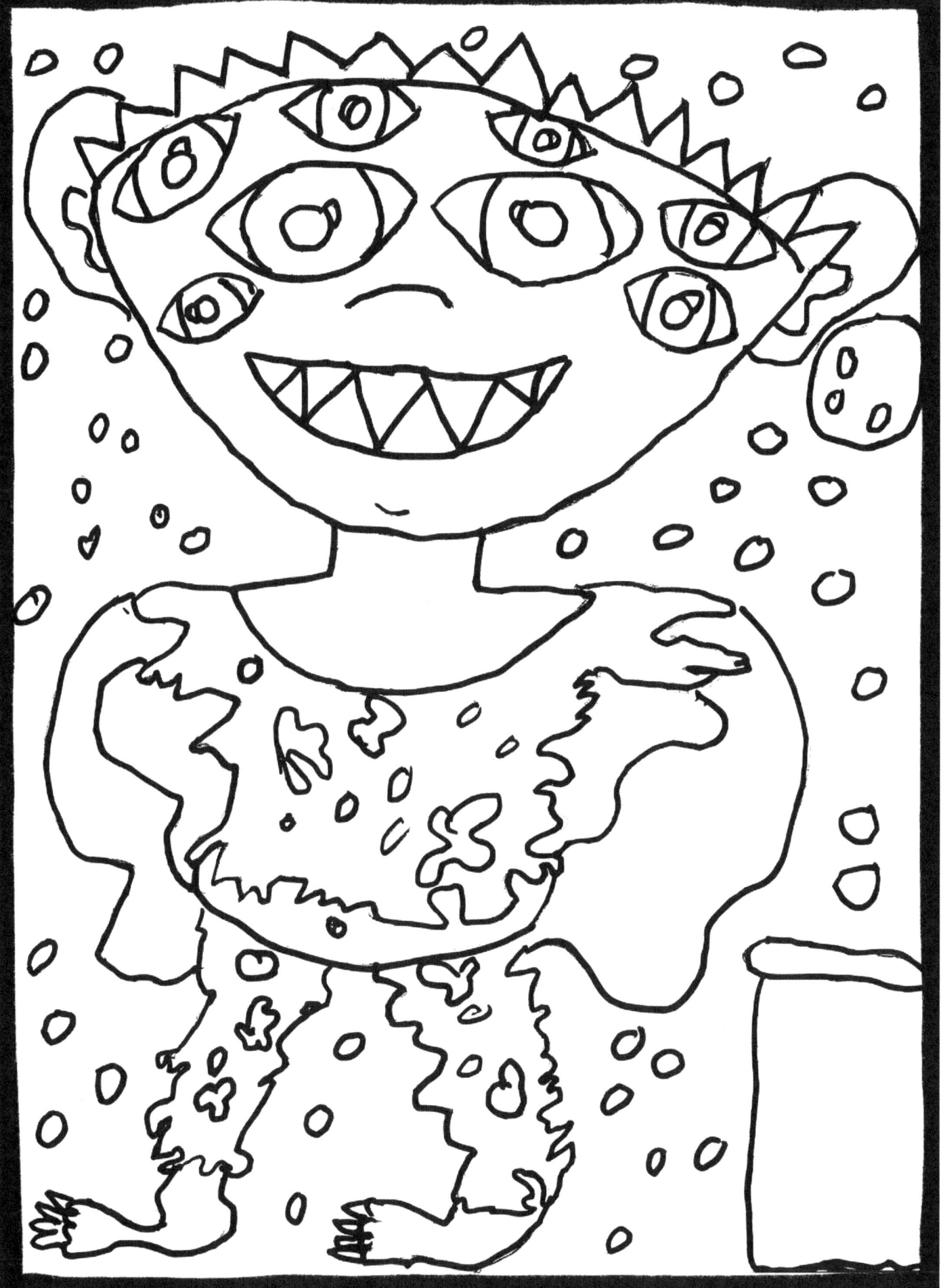

Blue Devil Pride

Caitlyn Fordyce
7th grade

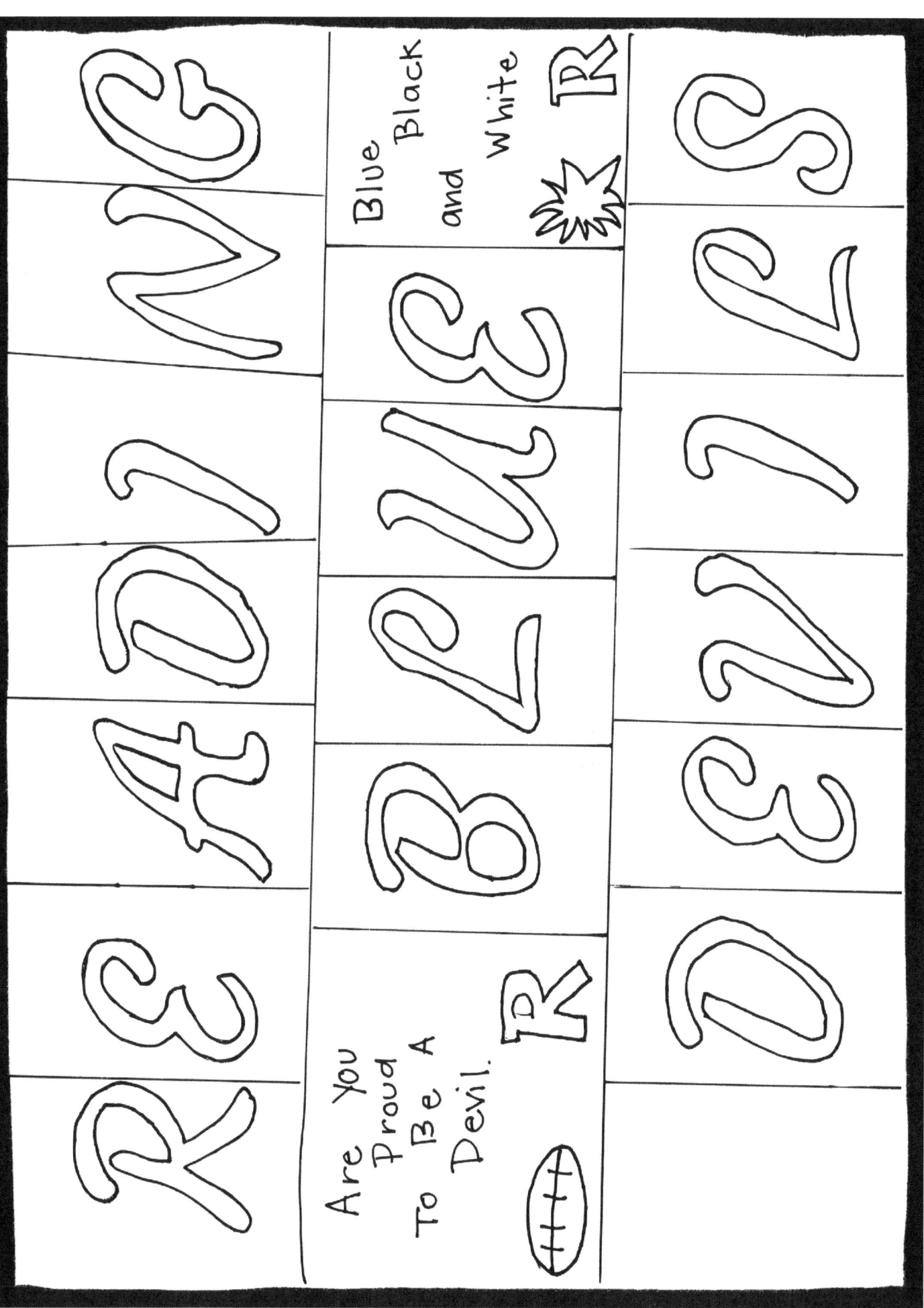

Is it Spring Yet?
Mrs. Nichols
2nd grade Teacher

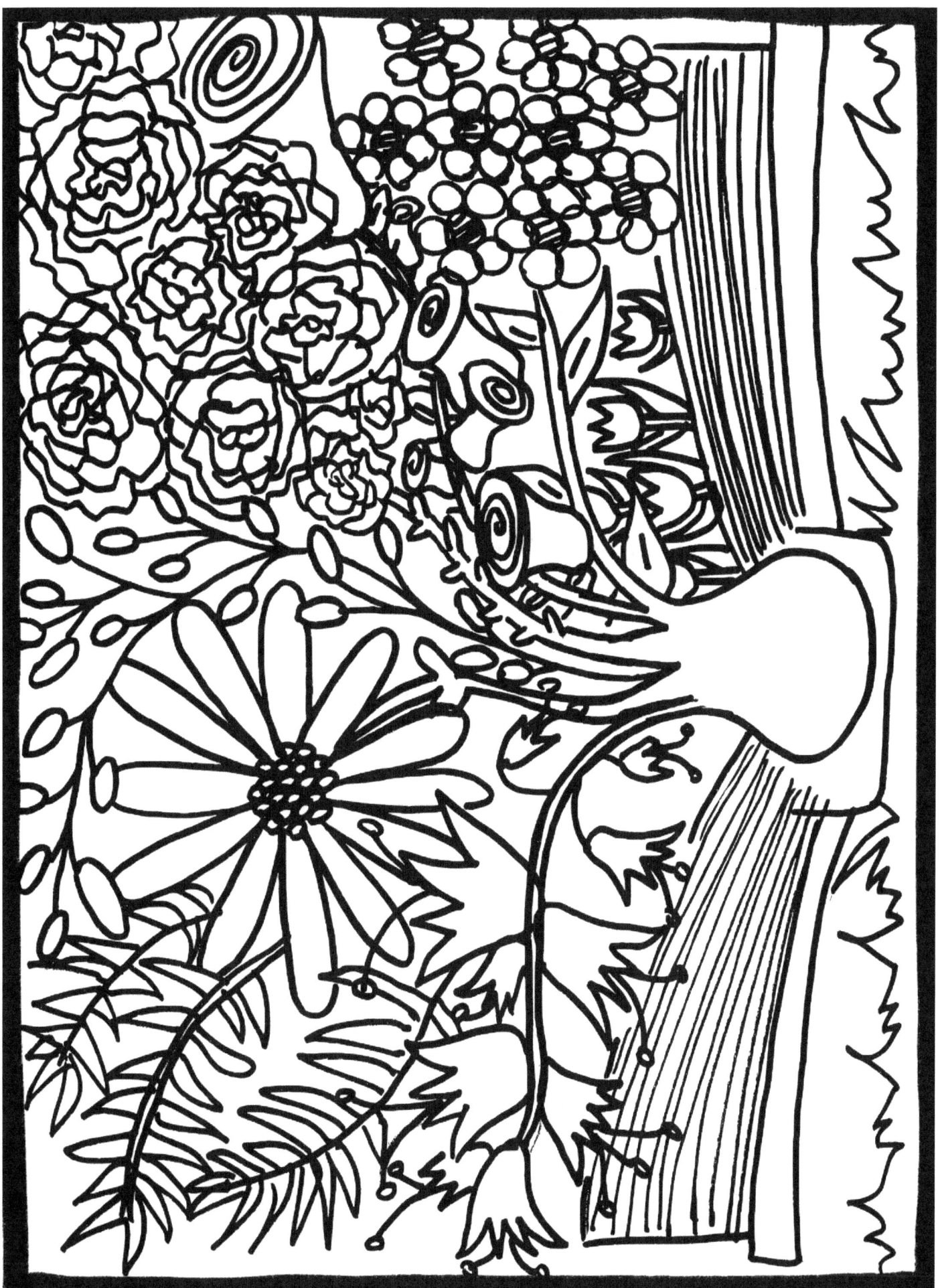

French Fry and Popsicle

Ava Ruff

4th grade

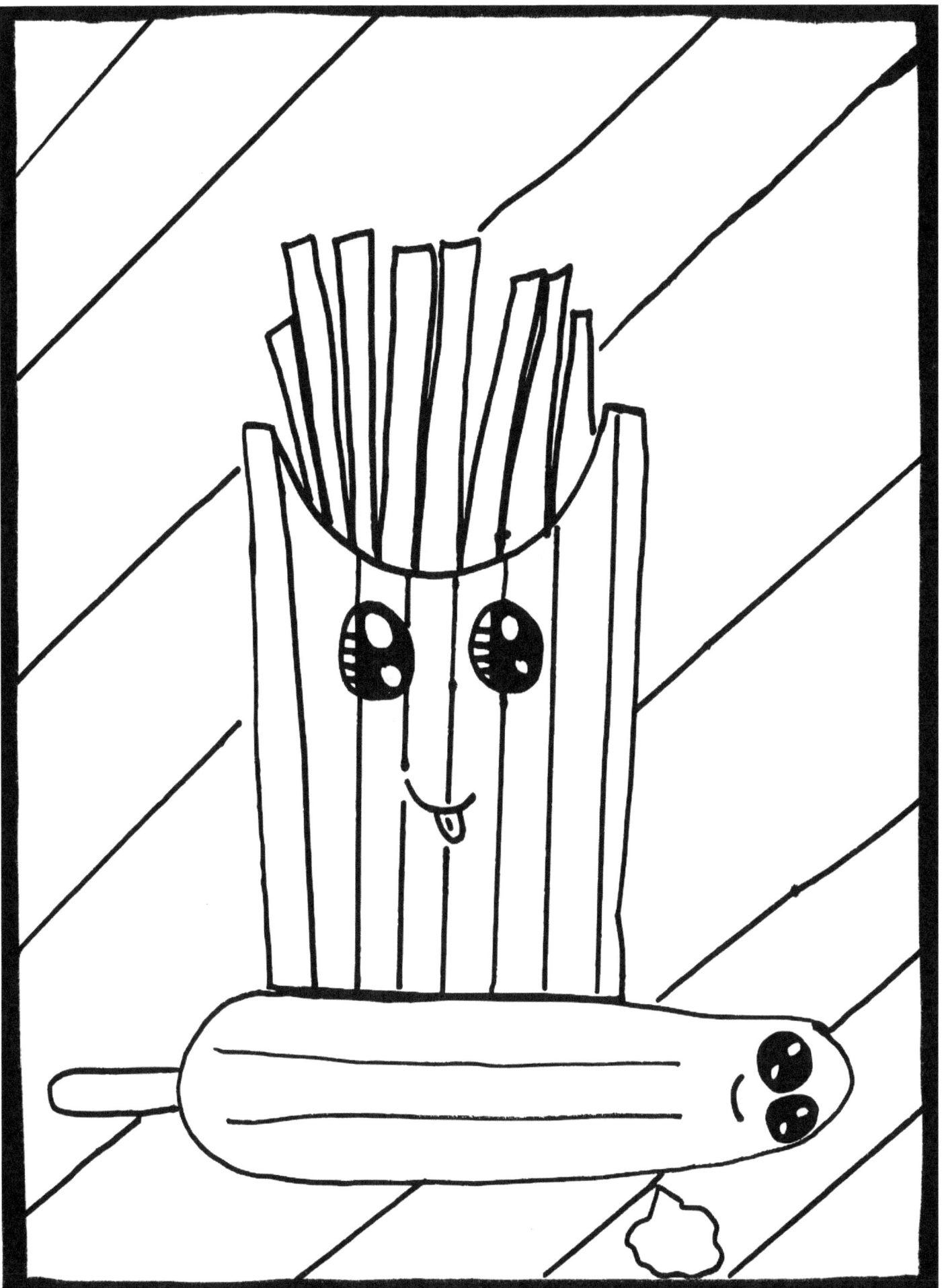

Bobby Bango Blasts Bluegrass From His Banjo

Mr. Schmidt
Elementary Art

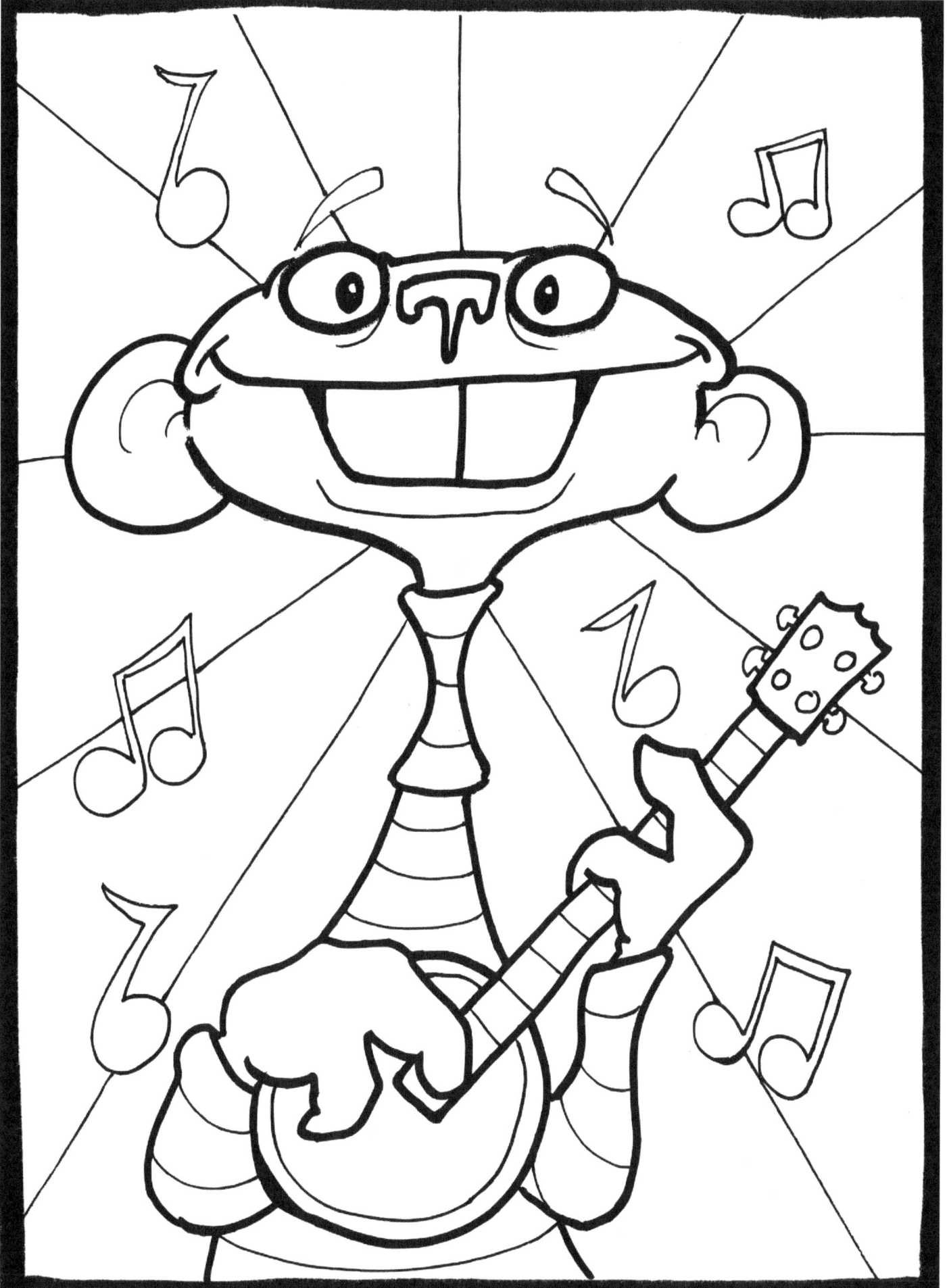

The Lonely Cat

Meredith Hess
3rd grade

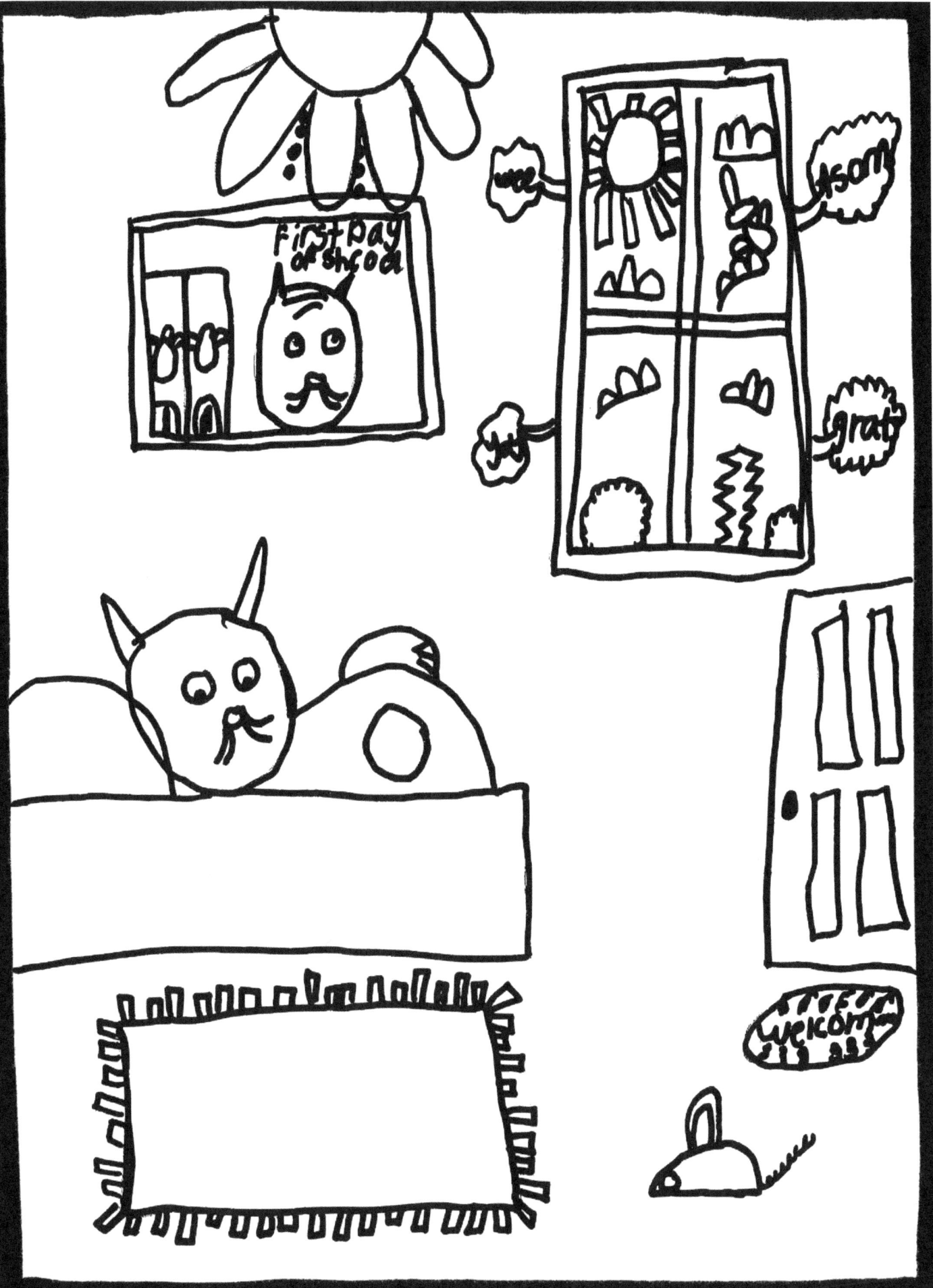

Untitled
Haley Brabant
11th grade

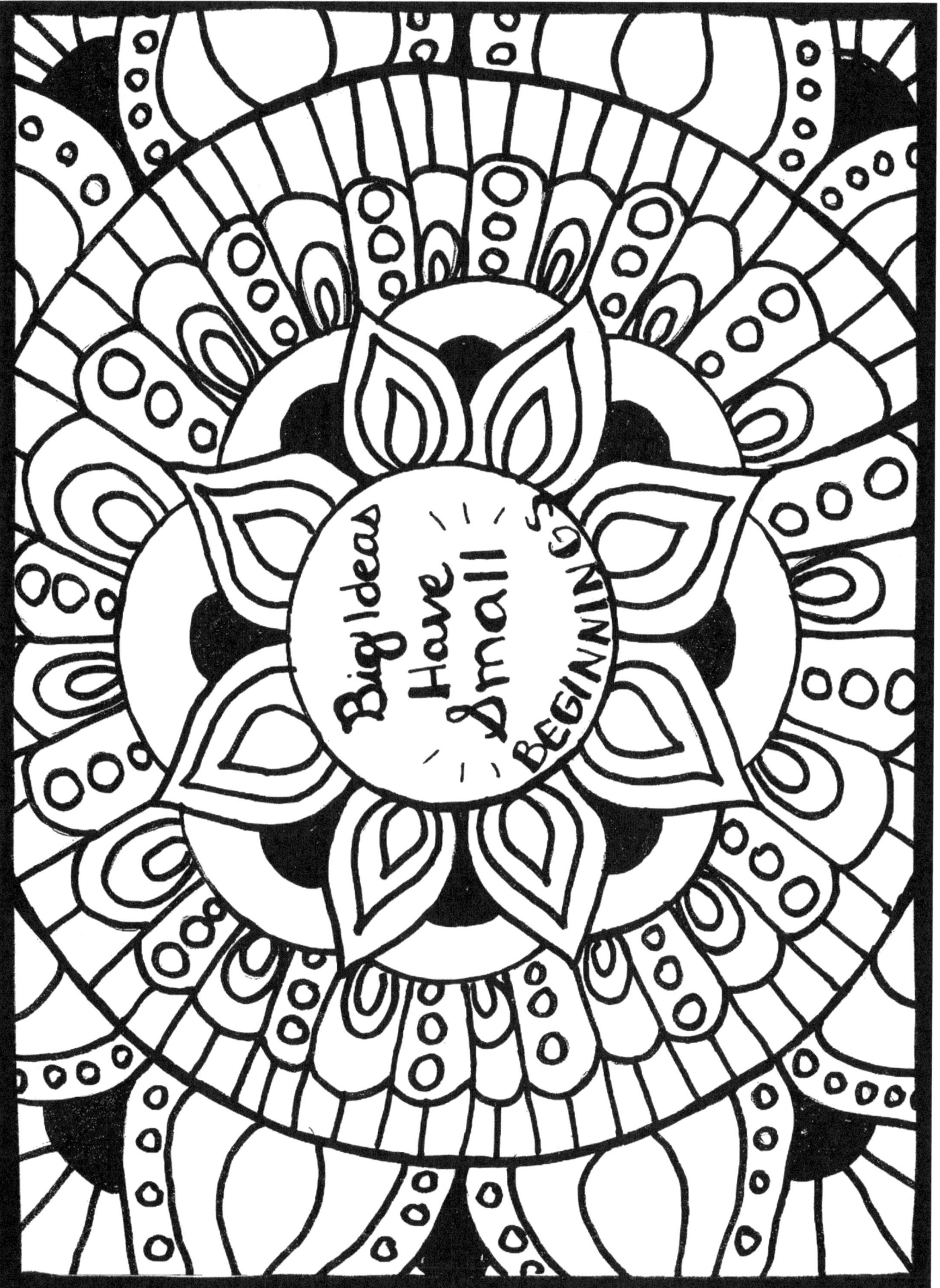

Reading's Blue Devil Cheerleader

Chris Zander
Parent

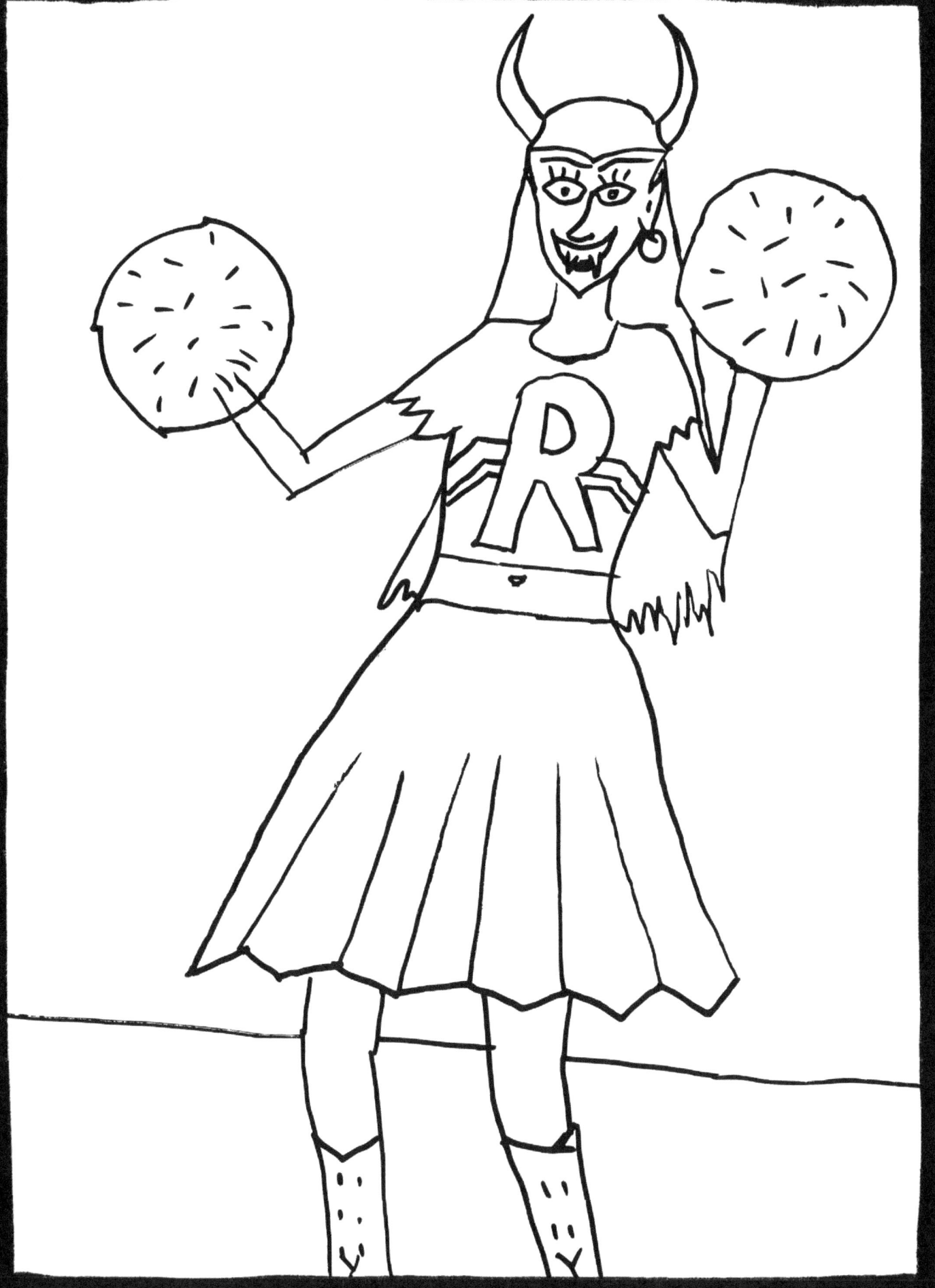

The Rain Fries

Ramata Anne
4th grade

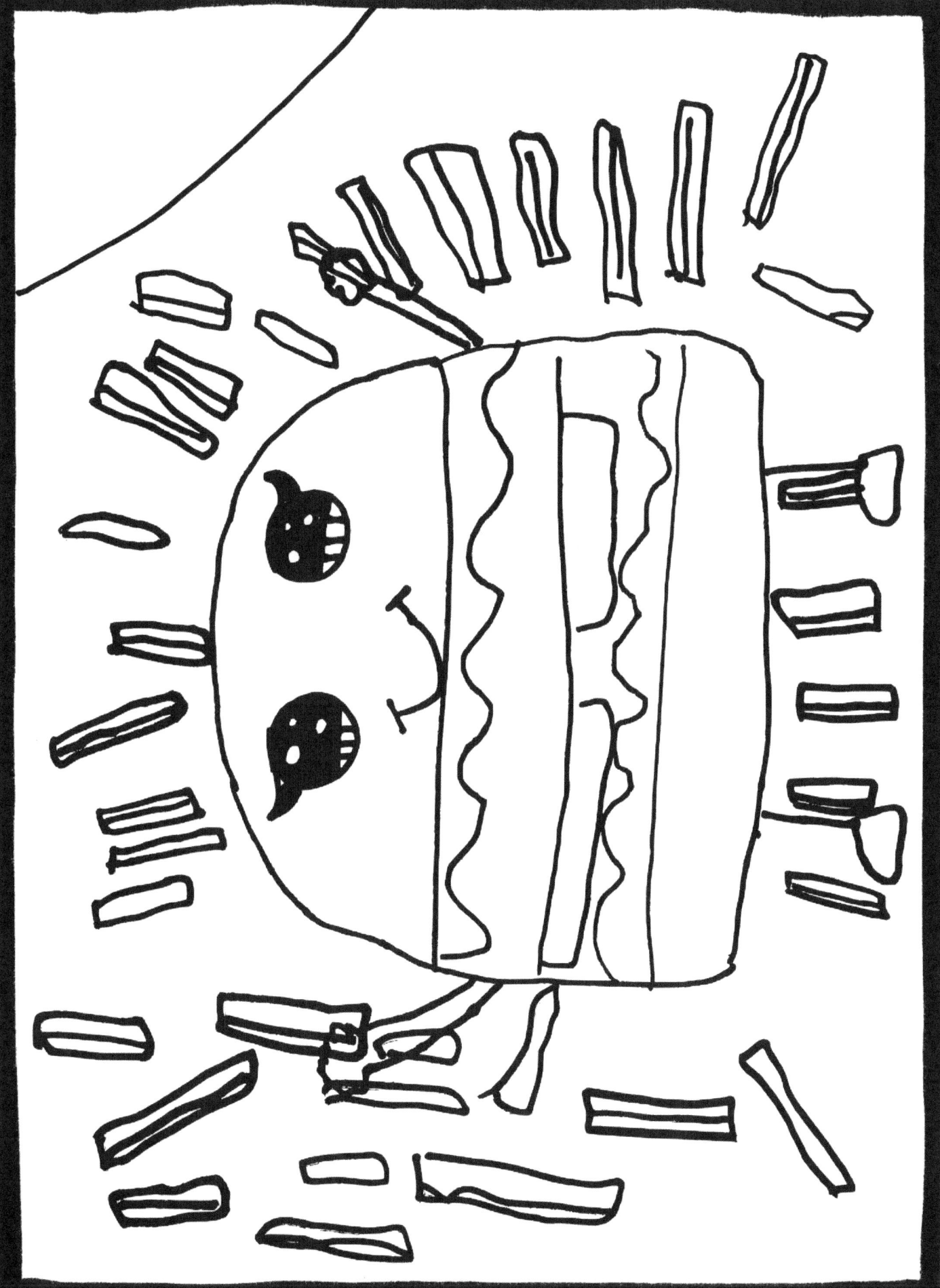

Yee Old Eel of Art
Ethen Miller
5th grade

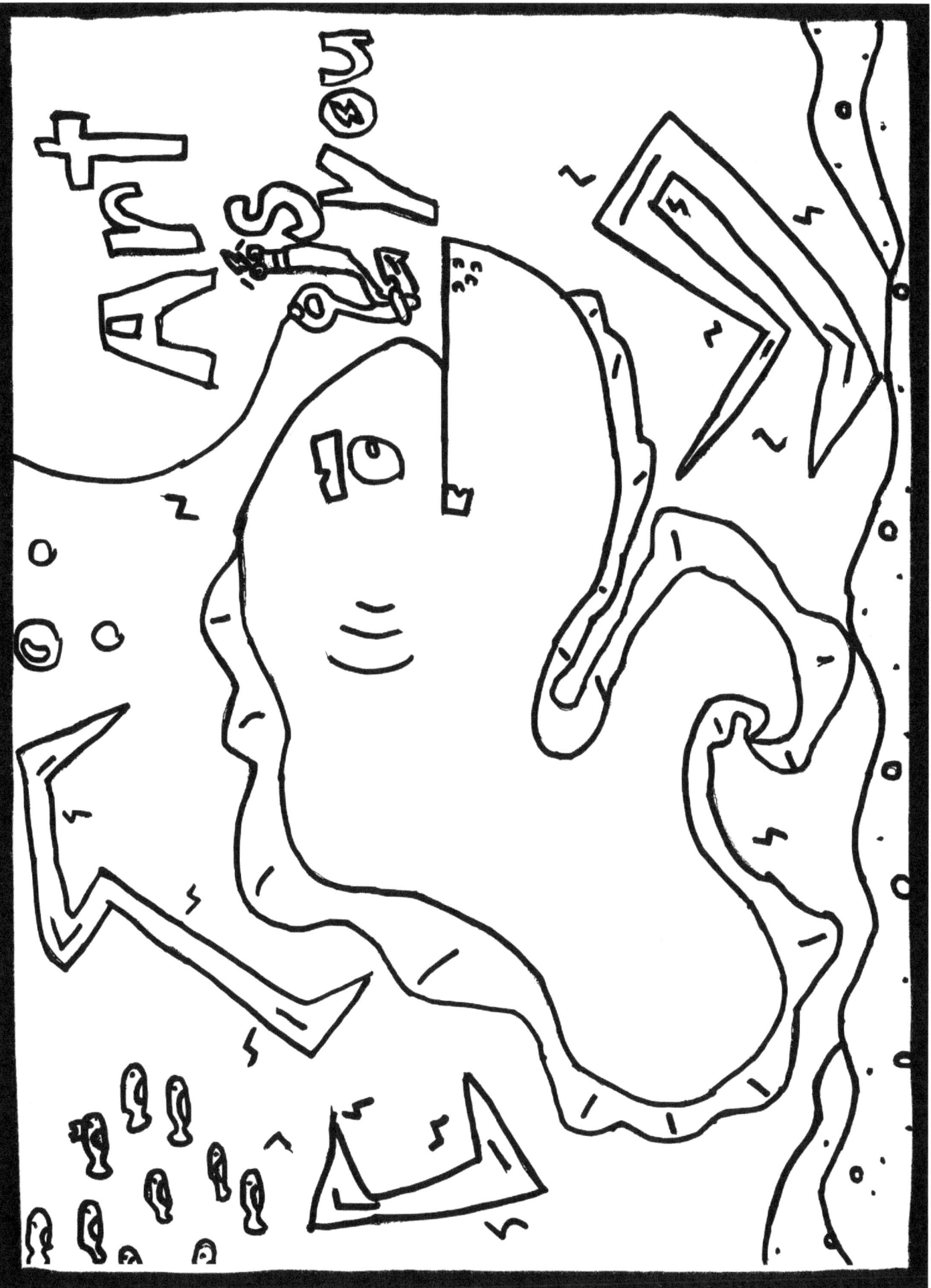

Reading Soccer

Olivia Simpson

7th grade

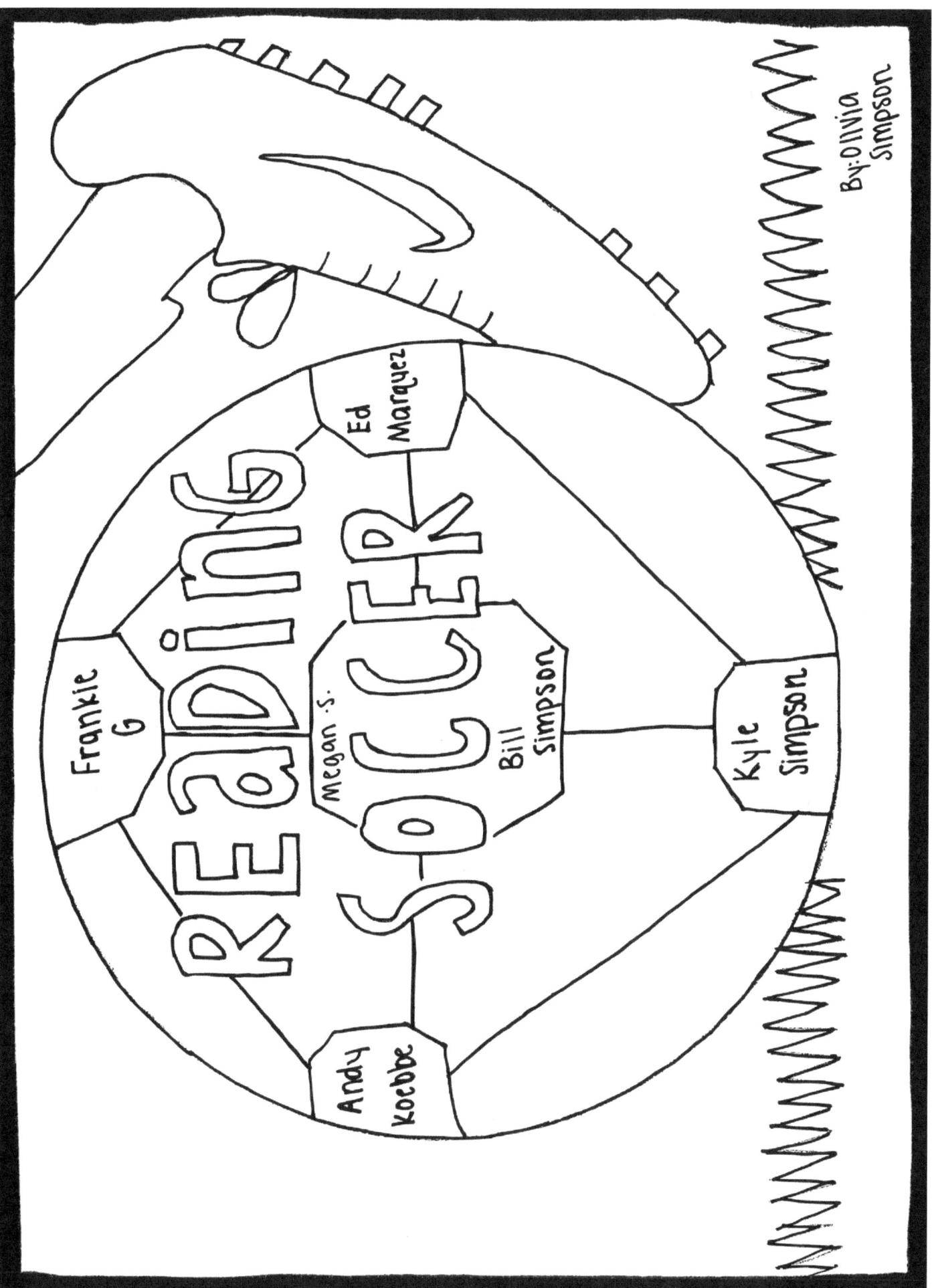

The Green Bunny

River Lay
3rd grade

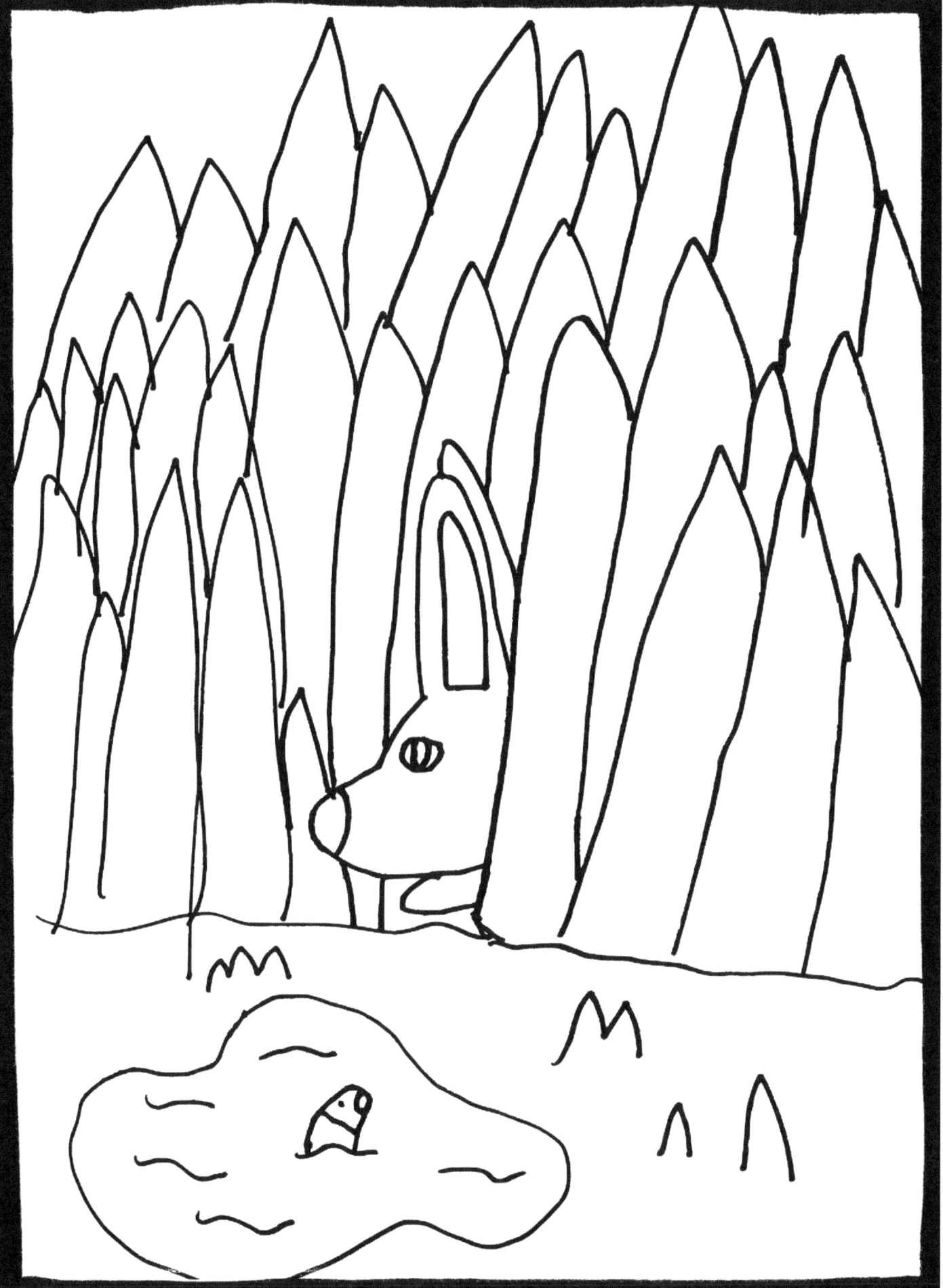

Battle of the Cretaceous Titans

Matt Rolfes
Local Artist

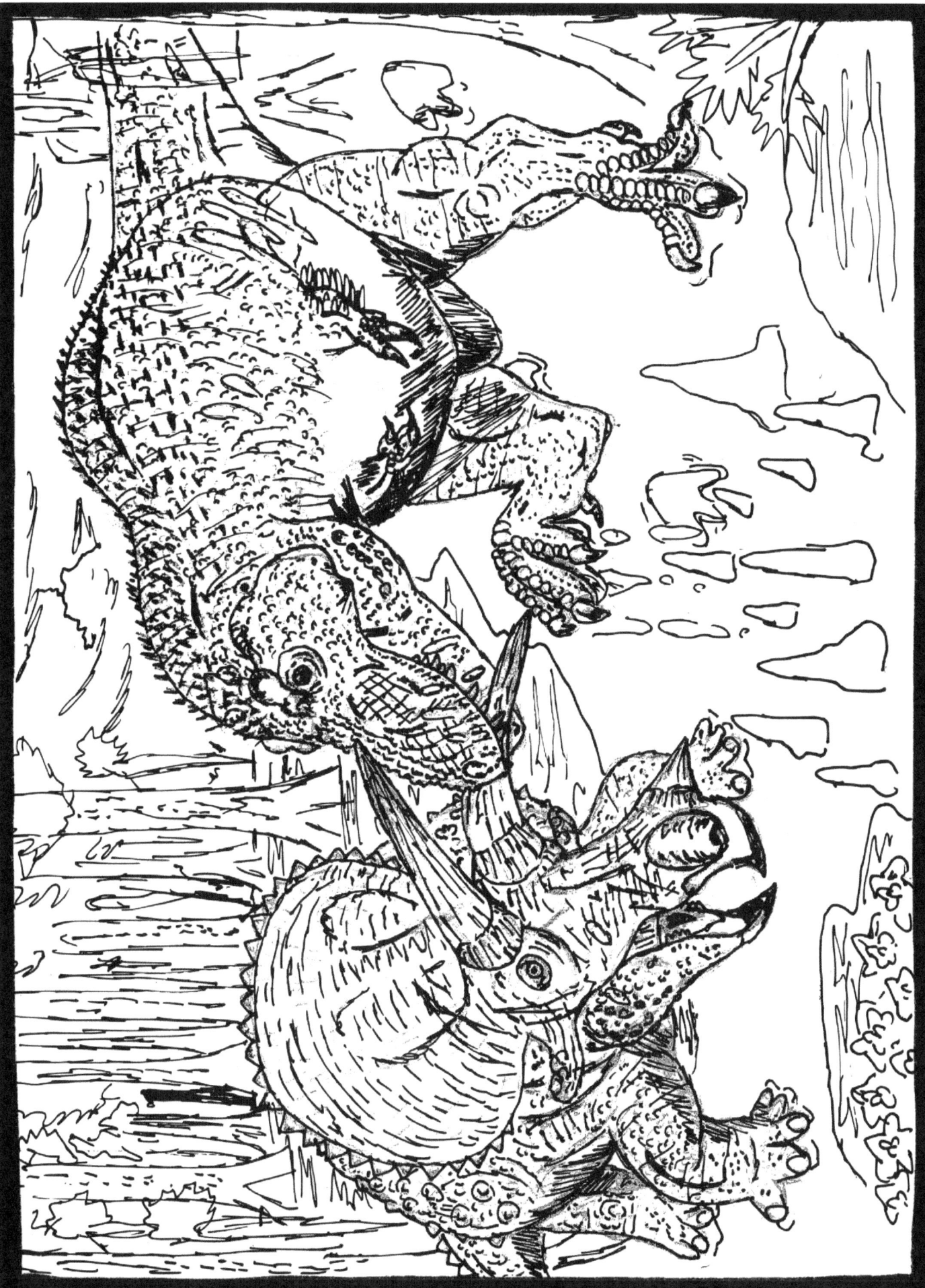

Create

Mrs. Freese
High School Art

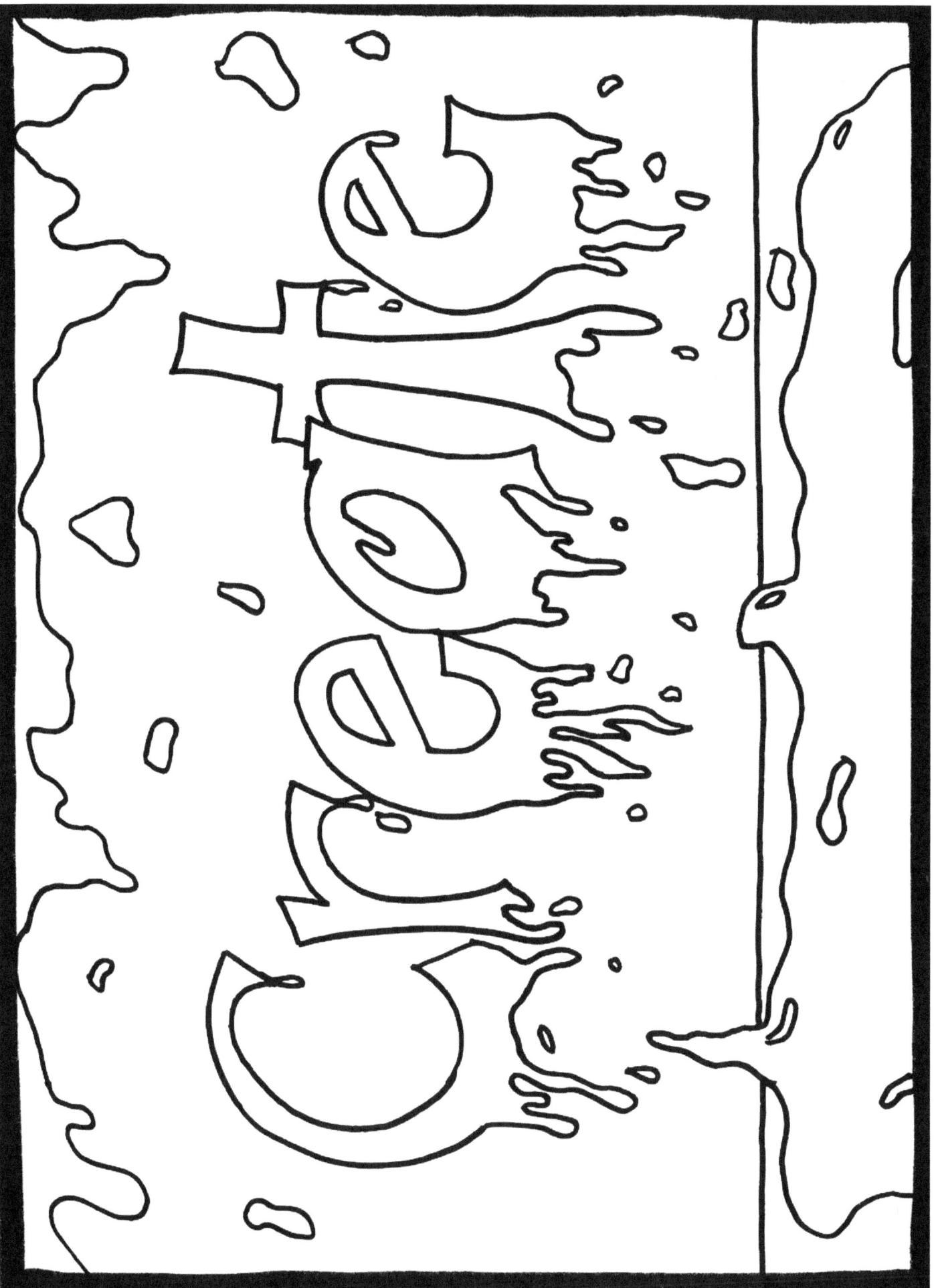

Fox's Starry Night
Jordan Chandler
6th grade

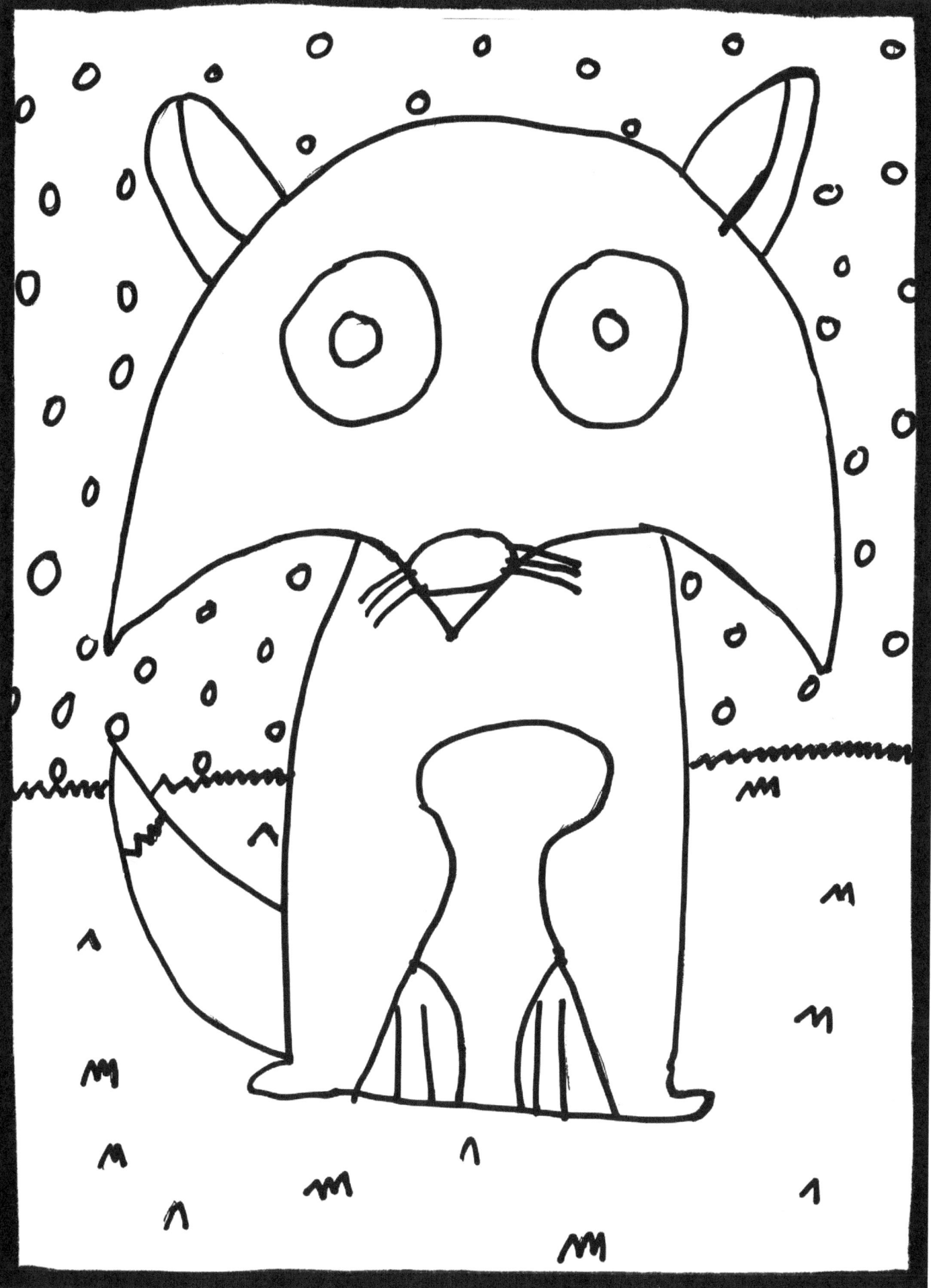

Zany Zentangle
Darian Barnett
Local Artist

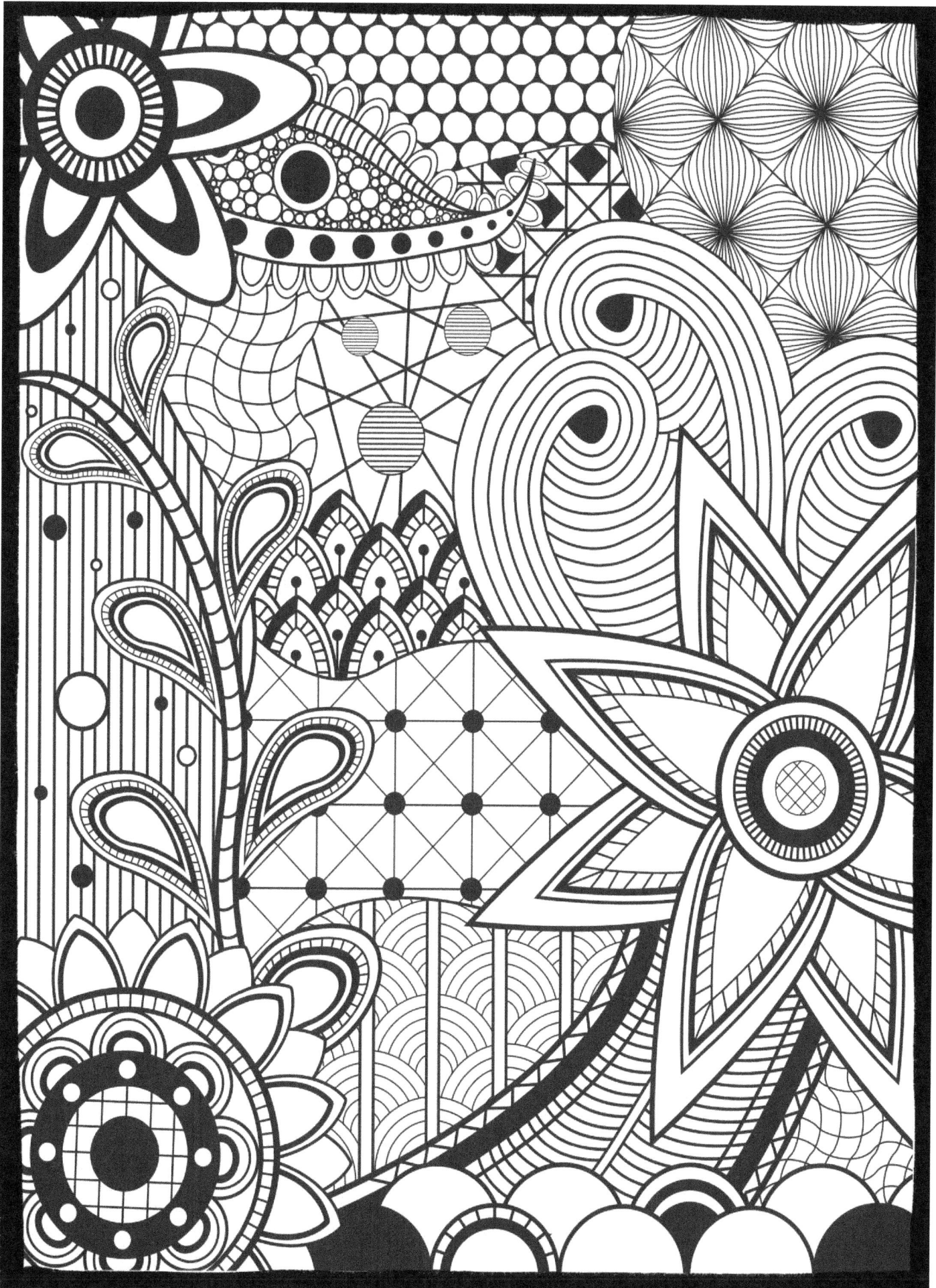

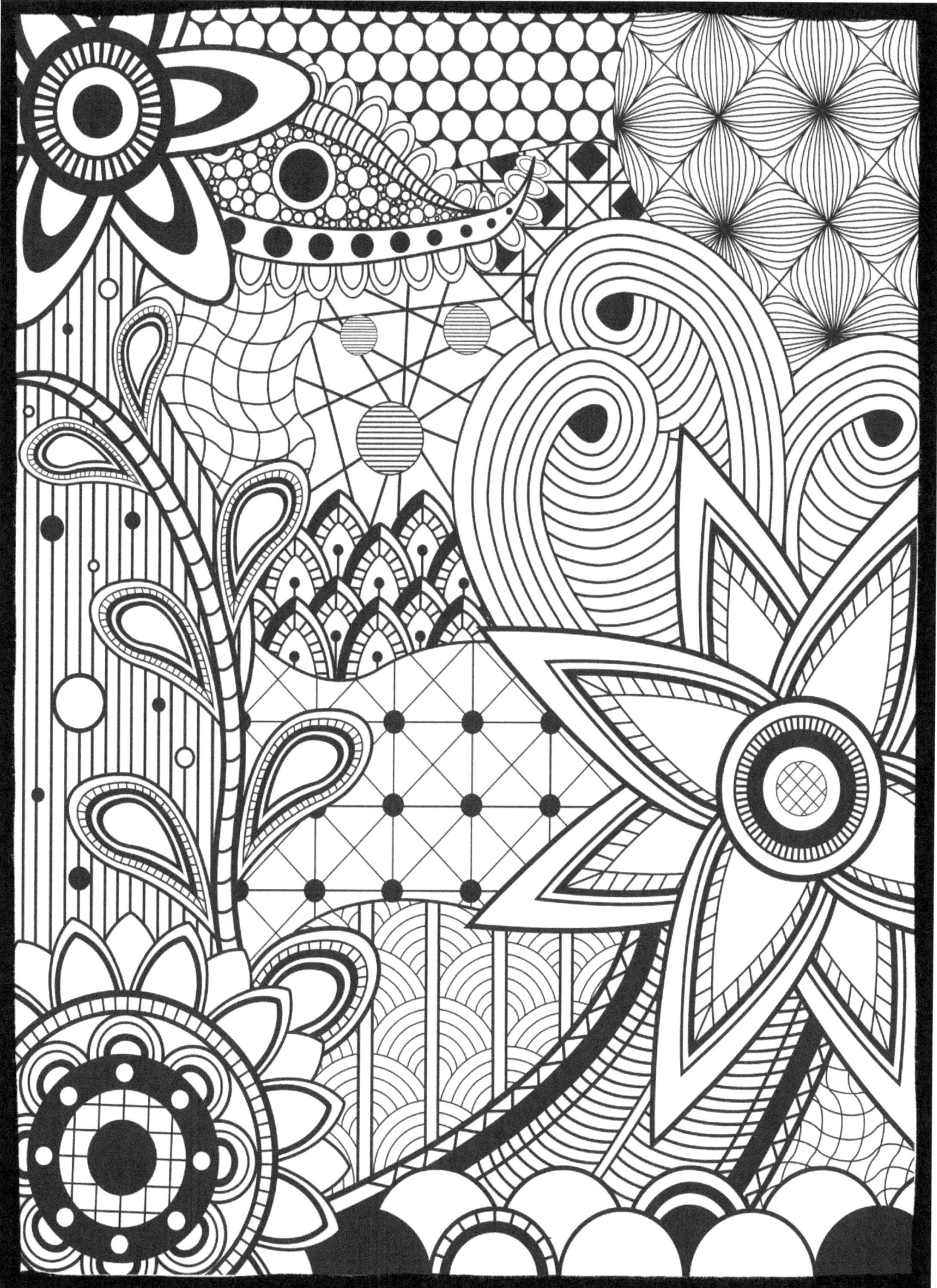

Copyright © 2018 Reading Encore

All rights reserved. This book or any portion thereof may not be reproduced or used in any manner whatsoever without the express written permission of the publisher except for the use of brief quotations in a book review.

Printed in the United States of America

First Printing, 2018

ISBN-13:
978-1986396769

ISBN-10:
1986396762

www.ingramcontent.com/pod-product-compliance
Lightning Source LLC
Chambersburg PA
CBHW062225220526
45471CB00009B/3354

www.ingramcontent.com/pod-product-compliance
Lightning Source LLC
Chambersburg PA
CBHW062225220526
45471CB00009B/3354